M000221980

For Mom, Dad, and Jen

PRAISE FOR
THE GOOD WAY

◁❚▢◉❚▢❚◉❚◉❚◉❚▢❚◉▢❚▷

"Evocative blend of ethnography and memoir, *The Good Way* is a revelatory account of a young woman whose questioning of rigid religious expectations leads her to undertake an anthropological pilgrimage to remote Himalaya passes, for which she is alone and scarcely prepared, but courageous enough to venture. As insightful as it is poetic, this book will be welcomed by anyone who has dared to seek, for a variety of social science and methodology courses, and by mountain lovers everywhere.

—*James Loucky*, Professor of Anthropology,
Western Washington University

"Brought up as a devout Christian, 17-year-old Julie Tate discovers the rituals and spirituality of other cultures on a missionary trip to India, and begins to doubt her and her family's devoutness to Christianity. Several years later, as an anthropology student, Tate's search to define her own spirituality brings her to the heart of the Himalayas of Nepal, where she treks alone to study isolated and unknown cultures hidden deep in the mountains. Heartbreaking, and beautifully written, *The Good Way*, chronicles a young woman's courageous quest to break with the past, make sense of a bigger world, and find her own god."

—*Lee Montgomery*, Author of *The Things Between Us*,
winner of the Oregon Book Award

"*The Good Way* is a heartfelt story of a young girl's quest for truth. At the vulnerable age of nineteen, Julie Tate leaves her safe home in Washing State and treks halfway around the world to answer the question that tugs at her soul. Living with villagers in the Himalayas, Julie compares her strict Christian teachings to the more flexible faiths Hinduism and Buddhism. Trekking alone across the tall mountain peaks, she endures the wilds of freezing temperatures, illness, and rushing rapids. She must decide whether God lives between the pages of her bible or somewhere inside a Buddhist temple. Throughout the pages of *The Good Way*, Julie shares her most intimate fears while facing life-changing events. Julie must either accept her life and return home to her Christian faith or be brave enough to embrace a new spiritualism. She does so by seeking the answer to one of the most difficult of questions of all times: Where does God truly exist? *The Good Way* is a must read that will enlighten any heart."

—*Lynn Yvonne Moon*, Author of *Whispers* and *The Tower*

The Good Way:
A Himalayan Journey

by Julie Tate-Libby

© Copyright 2019 Julie Tate-Libby

ISBN 978-1-63393-839-7

All rights reserved. No part of this publication may be reproduced, stored in a retrieval system, or transmitted in any form or by any means—electronic, mechanical, photocopy, recording, or any other—except for brief quotations in printed reviews, without the prior written permission of the author.

Published by

 köehlerbooks™

210 60th Street
Virginia Beach, VA 23451
800-435-4811
www.koehlerbooks.com

THE GOOD WAY:

A HIMALAYAN JOURNEY

JULIE TATE-LIBBY

VIRGINIA BEACH
CAPE CHARLES

PROLOGUE

◁❘▢◉❘▢❶◉❘◉❶◉❘▢❶◉▢❘▷

Solu Khumbu, Nepal: 1996

ALONE, I STARE DOWN at the snakelike river far below. The noonday sun bakes against my raw skin. Closing my eyes for just a second, I strain to hear the rushing water. Nothing. I'm too far away. Too high up. The sound of scuffling feet makes me turn. I almost laugh as an old man with bare feet, carrying a basket of wood upon his head, limps slowly toward me. He's the only person I've seen for hours.

"Please," I say. "How long to Sete?" Holding out the map, I run my fingers over the small letters. "Sete." I point to the word.

The old man frowns and shakes his head. "No, Sete, *didi*. Pike!" He pronounces it like the ballet term—*piqué*.

"Pike?" I repeat in a shallow whisper.

Wiping the sweat from my forehead that threatens to sting my eyes, my heart pounds. Glancing around, all I see are snowy mountaintops. A light breeze feels cool against my flush skin.

"Yes, Pike!" He points up the trail. "Pike, Pike!"

I take in a deep breath and let it out slowly. *Why won't he listen to me?* I shake my head. "No. sir, please. Sete. I must go to Sete."

The old man coughs a few times before spitting into a bush. Glaring at me through deep-set eyes, he frowns. The dirty creases on his face look shiny in the hot sun. I jump as he yells out the word again: "Pike!"

I shake my head again. Ignoring me, the old man turns to go. I gaze down at my map. I search for any place that starts with a *P*, but there is nothing. Holding back tears, my hands shake as my feet throb. *What do I do now?* I wonder.

"Sir! Please, sir!"

The old man shakes his head and points to the sky. "Pike . . . Pike . . . Pike . . ." He says it as if he's repeating a mantra, not talking to me.

Placing my hand over my chest, I say a small prayer. Obviously, I've taken a wrong turn and I'm not where I'm supposed to be. Squinting at the wrinkled paper, I try to make out the trail between the frayed folds. Perhaps it doesn't cross here. Maybe it continues along the river. Perhaps I have no idea where I am.

It's getting late. I must've been climbing for hours. Even if I turn back now, I'll never make it to that small village before dark. My headlamp is a dim little thing with weak batteries. There's no way I can find the trail in the darkness. One wrong step and it's a thousand-foot drop to the Himalayan River. A wave of panic washes over me.

I glance up the trail. The mountain seems to disappear into the sky. I have no idea how far I must climb. A deep rumble from far away means only one thing: a storm. All around me, mountains burst into the sky like flowers blooming on a summer day.

I'm nineteen.

I'm alone.

I'm lost in Solu Khumbu.

CHAPTER ONE

⊲❚▢◉❚▢❚◉❚◉❚◉❚▢❚◉▢❚⊳

Andhra Pradesh, India: 1994

IT WAS THE SCENT that I fell in love with first—the thick, hot rotting scent of human flesh and waste mixed with jasmine and red clay. It pervaded everything. It was the first thing to hit me, walking off the airplane on the tarmac under a blazing blue sky. Even as we left Delhi by train, it remained with me. Through Agra and Jaipur and the dark, rainy jungles of Bhopal and Indore, the scent carried me along. When I woke at night, unable to remember where I was, it brought me back to the rattling train. It followed me over hills and valleys until I arrived in the flat expanse of Southern India. From here we would begin our mission.

I couldn't shake the odor. It clung to my skin and leached into my hair. I could almost taste it, as if it had become a part of me. As I drifted in and out of sleep on the foam mats under the pink mosquito netting, it remained in my dreams—always, always, the cloying scent of flesh and waste and sweetness. Months later, no matter how many times I washed my clothes, that curious smell followed me. Many times, I pressed my skirt to my face and breathed in the aroma of India and the summer that changed my life.

I was seventeen that summer. Old enough to disagree. Old enough to wonder what we were trying to accomplish. India fascinated me. I loved the women with their bright saris and the tiny babies with dark eyes and tattooed hands. I loved the mud huts and red-clay roads, the villagers and the fishermen with their wooden boats. But what were we doing to them? When I first signed up for the trip, it seemed like the thing to do if you were seventeen and wanted to see the world. Missionaries were the only people I knew who traveled. My family attended a Nazarene church, and in our circles, no one journeyed far from home except for a second cousin. She was a missionary in Chad, Africa. She visited us once when I was about seven. The woman towered over me. She was so tall she had to duck as she entered a room. When she smiled, her big teeth flashed in her pale face. She wore purple African dresses with hand-carved wooden beads made by the women she worked with. I'd never met anyone like her. She was the most exotic person I'd ever seen. One night at church, she shared her slides with us. We watched as African children ate mealie meal from big round pots and attended a school she had started. Later, someone passed around an offering to support her work in Africa. After her visit, I daydreamed for hours about going to far-off countries. I, too, wanted to do good things like feeding orphans or teaching children.

On a snowy New Year's Day at my grandmother's house, I found a brochure on Teen Missions, an organization that took teens all over the world to spread the Good News. Maybe this was my calling. Maybe I could go to India and help those poor people.

In India, our days began at four in the morning. We were required to do personal Bible study, an hour of contemplative prayer and reading before breakfast. Stumbling through the darkness, with my Bible and journal clutched to my chest, I would climb to the rooftop to be alone with my thoughts. From there, I would look out over the landscape. It was quiet before the sunrise. No children crying in the distance, no donkeys braying. Only the occasional rooster broke the stillness. Before me, the desert stretched away flat and still, a drab gray-brown covered with scattered thorn bushes. In the gray light, I could just make out ragged clothes strewn over the bushes to dry. I sat with my legs crossed, looking at the pale eggshell-blue sky. The sun broke like water, spilling over the flat horizon, until it bounced up, hot and unforgiving—a bright bold eye in the middle of the sky.

Rules governed our daily activities. They governed our lives. *Do not walk outside the compound. Do not eat, write, read, or pray unless permitted to do so. No close friendships. No pairing off in small groups. Boot laces to be strapped. All thirteen hooks crossed and tied. No conversing with the locals without proper supervision.* On our daily trips to the villages, we were told what to say and to whom, what to wear and how, what to eat and when. How to think.

After breakfast, we climbed into an old army truck with a blue canvas cover. We sat in the back on two wooden planks, facing each other as the truck coughed to life, spewing diesel fumes and dust. The planks slammed against our bottoms. I liked watching the landscape disappear behind me. The roar of the truck made talking impossible. It was peaceful jolting along, waiting for the next village.

In the villages, huts made of mud and thatch lined the narrow streets. The villagers painted white chalk symbols in the dirt in front of their doorways to ward off evil spirits. The missionary leaders told us the signs were demonic. Some of the team members prayed for the villagers and their backward ways. I thought the symbols were beautiful. But I didn't say so.

The women stood in their doorways and stared at us missionaries. Babies coughed and cried on their hips. Orange saris covered their long dark hair. As I passed, they pulled their saris over their mouths and noses. Were they shy? Embarrassed? Some days, we were told to leave and go away. Some days, we stayed.

We rode in silence across that hot desert, and every day that unforgiving sun climbed higher and higher into the sky.

Our main goal was to convert the villagers to Christianity. We were supposed to be spreading the Word of God, like a farmer casting his seeds. We didn't know which seed might take root and find its way into someone's heart. *I* was never sure how a bunch of teenagers from the United States, who didn't speak the language, could convert someone. I wasn't even sure what that meant. But we persevered.

We spent most of our time performing skits. We worked hard on them. We staged them wearing black pants and purple T-shirts. Tape recorded music blared from an old cassette player on the back of the truck. With our hair pinned back and our faces painted white, we looked like professional street performers. Women gathered around, laughing and giggling, tucking their saris around their waists as their children hugged their legs. Silently, we acted out the story of creation, the crucifixion, Judas's betrayal, the Last Supper, and other Bible stories. Under that thick, oily white paint, my cheeks burned. I was a fraud. I didn't belong here, and I knew it. I felt sick with shame.

One day, we performed our skits at a village near the ocean. Under the hot sun, the water beckoned like a mirage. The beach was empty except for a group of fishermen, pulling their boats to shore. Catching sight of us, they came near. Staring, tilting their heads from one side to the other, they frowned. Their bare chests shone in the bright sunlight. They looked wild to me, with their strange faces and curly hair. Their hands were creased and calloused, probably from pulling ropes on the open sea all day. They stared at us.

At first, I thought they were just curious. Then one of them spoke loudly to James, our Indian interpreter. He frowned and shook his head. Did they want us to leave? We smiled and bowed our heads. We put our hands together in front of our faces and murmured a greeting in Telegu. *"Dūraṅgā uṇḍēvārini pilucuṭaku vāḍē ō śabdha viśēṣamu."* It was all they taught us to say.

The men talked rapidly, pointing to our clothes and our hair. One pointed at his face and shouted something. Maybe it was the white paint that bothered them.

"James," Lorena, a girl from our group, whispered, "what are they saying to you?"

James ignored her question. He continued to speak to the men in a calm voice. He pointed to the sky. I had no idea what he was saying. He spread out his hands and bobbed his head sidewise in the Indian style of acquiescence. The fishermen nodded, but their gaze felt hostile. One of the fishermen stood on one leg, balancing like a thin stork. He scratched his head. Seconds passed. We held our breath. After a while, the fishermen relaxed and walked back to the beach. Their voices, quick and unintelligible, floated through the air. They gathered their nets and pushed their boats into the water. They were gone.

Obviously, they did not want us there. Watching the men paddle into the open waters, I breathed a sigh of relief.

Lorena, who spoke earlier, asked James, "May we go swimming?"

The water sparkled in the afternoon sun; the waves looked sluggish and milky. I could almost feel the cold against my hot skin. None of us had showered in weeks.

James glanced at the water. "Why not?" He smiled at us.

We had no bathing suits, but we weren't allowed to expose our skin anyway. One by one, we took off our boots and ran to the water's edge. The others jumped in first, but I lingered on the shore, watching the fishermen as they cast their nets into the water. The sun glinted against the waves. I could just make out their little boats bobbing far out in the shining ocean.

My feet sucked in the wet sand as I waded into the water. How I wished I could dive down and never resurface. With the water up to my waist, I was lighter. Even in the bulky clothes that swirled around me, I felt buoyant and free. Suddenly, everything was alright again.

There was nothing but water—cool, lovely water—and open blue skies. For a moment, I felt normal—just a girl swimming in the ocean. I could almost forget where I was, forget the filth and mosquitoes, the canned food, and the laboring Bible meetings. Treading my bare toes, I could forget about the malaria or the squatty potties. I could forget the angry missionary leaders and the constant chattering. Out here, I was alone.

And, for one brief moment, I could forget the growing sickness in the pit of my stomach that nagged at me because I did not belong here, doing whatever it was that we were doing. I knew now that it was wrong. *Very wrong indeed.*

We swam for hours that day. We swam until the sun began to sink along the horizon, until the fishermen in their little wooden boats drifted back to shore, tossing silvery fish and calling to one another in the gathering dark. Sometimes, even now, when I think of India, I think of the way it felt to float on my back in the Bay of Bengal. The bright, hot sun and the waves, rocking me out to sea.

The locals—Jessie, Kamala, and James—felt sorry for us. They were born and raised in the nearby town of Vijayawada. They had worked with the missionary group for several years. All three men were gentle and funny. They made us laugh. Every morning, they visited some of us girls for breakfast. They snuck us juice packs and sweets when our chaperones weren't looking. At night, we ate the treats on our sleeping mats, looking up at the stars.

I always believed those men were in love with us. I still have the letters Jessie wrote to me. We were young American girls, silly, homesick, and exuberant. We all got love letters, which we read in the dark, whispering about how we would come back here one day on our own. Maybe we'd marry them and live in India for the rest of our lives.

Marlena, from Texas, had big sad eyes. She liked Kamala. Lorena had round rosy cheeks and a turned-up nose. She liked James. Blond-haired Holly had a restless spirit and an angelic smile. Holly and I both liked Jessie.

At night, we sat on the wall that surrounded our compound and fantasized about escape. We could walk through the desert, we said.

"We'd have to leave in the night," Marlena whispered.

"And steal back our passports," I said.

I imagined running over the moonlit scrub, tripping over roots and hiding in the bushes until daybreak. We would just keep going, we said. We could definitely make it to Ongole before heading south. We had seen the lights of Sri Lanka from the beach with the fishermen.

"We could steal a fisherman's boat," I said. I pictured the ones we'd seen that day, hollowed out by hand with the nets coiled at the bottom. "We could paddle to Sri Lanka."

"Yes, Sri Lanka," Holly said.

We would go to Sri Lanka and be free at last.

It was almost morning. Soft gray light showed along the horizon. We had whispered away the night. The monsoon rains drifted overhead, splashing our hot, feverish skin with fat water drops. We tiptoed into the courtyard and pulled on our boots. We gathered our bags and stole some bread. We couldn't find our passports, but we didn't care. What could anyone do to us?

We climbed up the courtyard wall and jumped down. The ten-foot drop surprised us in the dark. We stumbled. When our boots hit the soft sand, we ventured across the field. The thorns tore at our clothes. In the distance, we saw lights.

"Just keep going," I said.

"Yes," Marlena said. "Keep walking."

It was cool, in the darkness, before the morning. Dogs barked in the distance. Our hearts pounded.

From somewhere far away, temple bells rang. The strange, sad singing of the priests as they began their day with prayers to Krishna sent chills down my back. As the morning light lit the ground, we stared at each other. We were standing a mile away from our compound in a field with cows and wild goats. Piles of cow dung lay everywhere. Our courage melted.

"Maybe tomorrow," Holly said.

"Yes," I whispered. "Tomorrow we'll escape."

Together, we ran back to our compound. Stifling giggles, we helped each other over the wall. We lay on our sleeping mats and tried to control our breathing, as one by one, the rest of the team awoke. The day had begun.

The next day, we did not escape. Nor the day after that, nor the day after that. We survived our ordeal by reading poetry or writing in our journals. At night, after the missionaries went to bed, we climbed to the rooftop and lit candles. We called it our secret poets' society. Night after night, on that rooftop we told each other that God was bigger than the missionaries and bigger than us. We memorized each other's poems and wrote new ones—terrible poems about the boyfriends we missed and about India and the children with sores and the lepers with cataracts. We told stories about home and about what we would do with our lives when we returned. Maybe we would travel together. We would do great things with our lives; we just knew it.

One night, shortly after we'd arrived in India, I followed Kamala back from the market. We had gone for medicine, as one of the team members had a high fever. The stars shone in the velvety sky. I could just make out Kamala's white shirt a few feet in front of me. He hummed quietly to himself, swinging his arms at his sides. Across the field, a campfire flamed in front of a stage. A small crowd of people had gathered, and more kept coming.

"Wait, Kamala." I hurried to catch up with him. "What is that?"

Kamala kept walking. "Nothing."

I heard voices. It was strange. Not singing, but more tonal, rising and falling in one syllable. I'd never heard anything like it. Even in the hot night, their sounds made me shiver. It reminded me of birds in the forest.

"Is it singing?"

"It is nothing." Kamala waved his hand in the air. "Old songs." He stopped walking. We stood in the darkness, listening.

"What are they saying?" I asked.

"No one knows."

I stared at the fire. "They don't know what they're singing?" I said, intrigued.

"No." Kamala shifted, impatient. "They just learn the syllables and repeat them. Come," he said. "Let's go."

I stood there wishing I could go on listening forever. The voices were deep and primal.

Something about the chanting and their incomprehensible syllables reminded me of a church service I attended the previous winter in Canada. Christians call it the Toronto Blessing or the Holy Laughter Movement. I was curious about it, and Jack, a boy I liked, was going, so I rode along.

When I arrived at the church service with Jack, people were everywhere. Some rocked back and forth, singing with their eyes closed. Others lay on the floor, crying or laughing. They appeared to be in some kind of a trance. A few sat in chairs with their heads bowed while people in white shirts prayed over them.

I stood near the back, my heart thudding. Jack moved to the front of the crowd, leaving me alone. I stood there, wondering what to do. A bald-headed man with a shiny face smiled at me. Holding firmly to my arm, he guided me toward the stage, where people gathered for *the blessing*.

On stage, a band played soft music and a man sang into the microphone. Every so often, he'd lean over someone in line and place his hand on their head. Everyone had their eyes closed, their hands folded, waiting for the blessing. I shifted nervously, peeking from the corners of my eyes. The worship leader was only two people away. I shut my eyes and tried to relax. Feel the presence. Feel the Spirit. The lady in front of me gave a soft cry and fell to the floor. Several men rushed up and pulled her away. I was next. After handing the microphone to an attendant, the worship leader reached out and touched my shoulder. With his other hand, he touched my forehead.

I stared up at him. He stared back, his eyes vacant and strange. Was I supposed to fall to the ground too?

I couldn't move. My heart pounded. The floor seemed to fall away. Then it was over. Nothing happened. There was no divine presence, no spirit, no revelation. The man moved on, touching the girl next to me. She fell to the floor like a stone. People sobbed, their gazes transfixed with joy. A woman on my left jumped up and down. Her hands fluttered like little birds, babbling something that sounded like *"Eh, Elioweh, Eh Elioweh, alieha, alieha, elowhim"* over and over. I closed my eyes and found myself crying hot, sticky tears. I didn't know why.

It was hot that night in India. Even in the darkness, the air felt heavy and suffocating.

"Come," Kamala said, motioning for us to go. We left the fire and the singing and hurried along the empty road.

Later, back at the compound, I could still hear the singing. The strange songs echoed throughout the night and into the early morning. The missionary leaders told us to pray to ward off the demonic spirits that had possessed the villagers. We sat in a circle and held hands. Together, we prayed.

Later, after everyone had gone to sleep, I climbed up the wall and listened to the wild singing of birds in the dark. I found it beautiful and haunting.

Years later, while attending graduate school, I studied ecstatic speech. Glossolalia was the spontaneous eruption of gibberish during heightened religious states. People exhibited symptoms of somnambulism, hypnotism, catalepsy, and hysteria. Reading about the different forms of ecstatic speech, I remembered the night in India when I listened from the rooftop. The village singers were Brahmins, a priestly caste. Although it sounded like gibberish to me, they were singing mantras, oral chants passed down from father to son. The mantras were first recorded in the late 1990s. Scholars discovered that the chants were old. The syntax followed no known human language. Computer analogs found the closest likeness came from forest birds.

That night in India in 1994, I did not know about any of this. I sat on the rooftop under a fat yellow moon, thinking about the strange religious service I experienced in Canada and the woman who shook her hands and danced.

What was the difference between the woman speaking in tongues, filled with the Holy Spirit, and these chanters singing to their gods in bird-tongue? Was one good and holy and the other bad and demonic? Was it the same, or was it different?

One day in late July, as we performed the Creation skit in one of the villages, I got ill. I had felt strange all week, but now waves of queasiness rolled over me. Spots swam before my eyes. I asked to be excused and headed back to the jeep near the entrance of the village. As I stumbled past a small bright-blue building, I heard singing. I glanced around. The missionaries were back in the village center; no one could see me. I stepped inside the courtyard. The heavy wooden door stood open. Cautiously, I tiptoed up the stairs. I peeked in. It took a few seconds for my eyes to adjust. Bold, colorful statues lined the walls. Half animal, half god, their garish grins and bulging eyes stared down at me.

Susan, our team leader, told us that Hindu gods were demonic. She warned us never to look directly into a god's face. It would pollute our minds. Demons were real. They could possess us at any time.

These were the first Hindu gods I had ever seen. I stood in the doorway, transfixed. Inside was cool and quiet. A priest hummed something that sounded like a hymn as he dusted the altars. Every few feet, he stopped and lit an incense stick at one of the figure's feet. *Grotesque*, I thought. But I couldn't rip my eyes away. There were so many of them. They were different colors and in different positions. Laughter. *Is that laughter?* A hollow, empty laugh echoed through the building, or was it in my head? Maybe the gods were mocking me with my missionary clothes and the Bible clutched in my hands.

I turned away. Black spots swam before my eyes. It was so hot. Now, the queasiness turned to nausea. Taking in a deep breath, I steadied myself. I couldn't be sick, not here. I had to make it back to the jeep. As I staggered down the dusty road, shading my eyes against the sun, it suddenly hit me. *I don't want to be here.* Skinny white cows wandered the street. Chickens clucked in the dirt. I could hear the priest chanting his prayers.

The rest of the summer stretched out before me in an endless stream of Bible studies, jeep rides, and prayer meetings. *I can't do this,* I thought. *I would rather die.* There it was in my head, clearly, almost in black and white as though someone had typed it across my eyelids. I wanted to die. I felt like I used to in junior high, fasting and watching my flesh disappear. I wished I could fade away into nothing; a none-being. I wanted to be a whisper, a fragment, a memory. Sometimes on the bus, on the way home from school when the boys were taunting me, showing pictures of porn and pretending to jerk off, I used to close my eyes and imagine myself shrinking away and disappearing altogether, evaporating like water droplets on a hot afternoon.

I could go dark, I thought. I could go still and dark so that nothing could touch me—not the Bible, not God, not the missionaries. Maybe not even my own sense of shame and self-loathing.

I would survive by not eating. I could stop eating and be thin again. Thin enough to disappear. It was lovely to be thin, lovely to disappear. When I didn't eat, it felt like a void. Everything became still and silent inside. Everything was beautiful and dark. It was just me and my body. No one could make me believe things I didn't want to believe. No one could touch me.

The next day, there was punishment. One of the missionary leaders had seen me in the door of the temple. They gave me the task of cleaning latrines. At our compound, our bathrooms were just two concrete stalls with holes in the ground. It wouldn't have been so bad had not everyone been sick. Today, the latrines were filthy. I scrubbed away layers of human waste with my bare hands. I carried the buckets of waste water out to the field. I burned baskets of used toilet paper. I was filthy. I stunk. But I did not care. I did what I was told.

That evening, I prayed the prayers they told us to pray. I sat in the circle. I closed my eyes. I memorized the verses. I sang the songs they told us to sing. I conformed. I gave in.

But inside, there was nothing. I felt nothing. Even when one of the missionary leaders berated me in front of the team, when she yelled until her voice cracked and her face went white with fury, I was curiously calm. When I lost even the privilege to sit on the rooftop, that too was okay because I had already retreated to a place where it didn't matter.

Once, when I was a little girl, my sister and I found a baby snowshoe hare. We wanted to save it. We made a home for it of straw and put it in our rabbit hutch. We gave it water and fed it lettuce. We offered it pellets of crushed alfalfa. The small creature sat in the corner and watched us, its brown eyes glistening. We held it and felt its tiny heart beating. We pressed it to our noses and talked to it. The next morning, it was dead. It lay curled up within itself as small as it could get.

In India, I learned that you cannot cage the spirit. The spirit is a wild thing. If you try to imprison it, it will flee or wither up and die. In the end, what I learned in India was not Christian. It was not Hindu or Buddhist or Islamic. Instead, it was the path of freedom, my freedom—and the beginning of my journey into the mountains.

CHAPTER TWO

◁□◉□◉□◉□◉□◉□◉□◉◉□▷

KATHMANDU, NEPAL: 1996

"TONIGHT IS KUMARI'S NIGHT," a mustached man called out.

I could barely make out his white T-shirt in the darkness as I followed him up the narrow, dusty steps. My legs wobbled. My head throbbed. Climbing four flights of stairs after a thirty- six-hour flight from Seattle to Kathmandu, I felt like I hadn't slept in years. We paused at the top of the landing.

"What night?" I asked, trying to catch my breath. *What is he talking about?*

"Kumari." The mustached man pulled a set of keys from his pocket. "Tonight is Kumari's night."

I had no idea who Kumari was, but she sounded exotic. Shifting my weight under my backpack, I watched the man fumble with the key in the lock. My cotton dress clung to my back in the still, hot hallway. At last, he pushed open the door, revealing a cloud of dust that hung in the late afternoon sunlight.

"Bed, bath." He pointed toward the narrow cot and a dark doorway. "Is okay?"

"Yes." I smiled weakly.

The mustached-man turned to leave and said, "Kumari, living goddess." I stared at him.

A living goddess? I wanted to ask more. He bowed and backed out of the room. Alone, I collapsed onto the thin, gray mattress, letting my pack tumble to the floor. A dirty white fan stirred the sticky air. I touched the wall closest to the bed. A fine layer of dust covered the peeling teal paint. On the opposite wall, a large, grated window faced the east. Rising, I walked to the window and peered into the street below. Women in bright saris and men in tattered shirts shuffled shoulder-to-shoulder. The huge crowd moved as one pulsing mass. I watched as pigs tossed their snouts before scampering away from the oncoming crowd. Even the pigeons scattered. Boys with thin legs and ripped T-shirts raced alongside, pelting each other with rocks.

I sat on the edge of the bed and pulled out my *Lonely Planet* guidebook. Flipping through the index, I searched for today's date. Tonight was the final night of Indra Jatra, a weeklong festival marking the end of the monsoons. It was dedicated to Kumari, the living goddess of the Kathmandu Valley.

Brushing the hair out from my eyes, my fingers caught on the limp strands. *When did I last shower?* My skin felt tacky; I could smell the airplane on my dress. My stomach clenched with hunger. Outside, the city rang with the sound of horns and drums. People shouted. *Is this real? Am I actually sitting in a guesthouse in the medieval city of Kathmandu?*

I had come to Nepal as a nineteen-year-old anthropology student on an independent study program from Seattle Pacific University. Seattle Pacific wasn't known for turning out anthropologists. It was better known as a place for Christian girls to find a good husband. I applied because a boy I liked attended the school. But I didn't fit in with the happy, well-adjusted kids from the prosperous Christian homes. I hated the weekly worship meetings and the mandatory churchgoing on Sundays. I felt like an imposter, a hypocrite. This quarter, I escaped to the most mysterious place I could think of: Nepal, the last Hindu nation on earth.

Now, on the fourth-floor of the guesthouse, I wondered what to do. Should I take a shower and go to sleep? I glanced at the bathroom. No shower, only a leaky faucet and a bucket with an oily bar of soap. That bucket bath could wait. Grabbing my notebook, I slung my purse over my shoulder and ran down the stairs.

The sea of bodies struck me like a wave. Pink-sari-covered backs pressed against me. Now, I was shoulder-to-shoulder with everyone else. Resolutely, the crowd moved toward Durbar Square. *What are we following?* Shading my eyes from the sun, I could just make out a procession of dancers in bright costumes with grinning masks and pointed headdresses. They twirled and somersaulted around four young men in ragged white shirts. The men carried a palanquin above their heads. Behind them loomed onion-domed spires and Azteclike temples silhouetted against the setting sun. I smelled the acrid scent of smoke from burning altars. We must be close.

We were following Kumari, the patron deity of Kathmandu and an incarnation of the Hindu goddess Durga. According to tradition, the living spirit of Kumari descends to a new girl every few years. The girl must never have shed blood. Kumari translates to "virgin" in Sanskrit. Even bleeding from a lost tooth is inauspicious. Therefore, the chosen girl must be young, usually five or six years old. Once found, the new Kumari takes up residence in an ancient wooden palace called Kumari Chowk. She lives in seclusion except on rare occasions like tonight, when she's paraded through the city on a palanquin and worshipped as a goddess.

Shuffling along with the crowd, I tried to get a glimpse of the Kumari. Kathmandu on any night would be chaotic, but tonight it was a cacophony of pipes, drums, and blaring music.

The muggy air tasted hot. I could smell food and sweat and the faint, ever-present hint of decay.

We entered a crumbling brick court lined with temples and spires. Street merchants with baskets of Tiger Balm, shawls, incense, and chess sets lounged inside the doorways, waiting for tourists to ply their wares. Women selling potatoes, lettuce, and plump tomatoes lined the crowded walkway. Two dancers with masks and elaborate robes capered on the steps of an ancient palace decorated with intricate wood carvings and latticework. Near the palace, an enormous statue of a face with huge lips, gaping white teeth, and bulging eyes stared down at me. I knew of this Hindu god. But seeing him in person was terrifying. A long tube protruded from his mouth. Clear liquid trickled from the plastic tube. It smelled sweet and alcoholic. Lines of small boys fought their way to sip a drink. They staggered away, giggling and laughing.

The crowd seemed to be growing. People moved in closer to me, shouting as the masked dancers pirouetted toward us. People chanted and pumped their fists into the air. The Kumari was close, but I couldn't see her through the crowd. I scrambled up the steps of the palace to get a better look. There she was. Her small, painted face and huge black eyes, thickly edged with kohl, peered out from layers of red robes. She looked like a doll, sitting there rigid and unmoving. She held her chin high, shoulders stiff, eyes wide and unblinking. A tall, red headdress with yellow tassels framed her face. She turned toward me. Her gaze looked foreign and strange. Our eyes met. Then she was gone. The dancers with their colorful masks and swirling arms led the way amid beating drums and clapping hands.

Virgin worship in Nepal dates back to the Malla dynasties when Rajput kings fled Muslim Turks in India and sought refuge in the Kathmandu Valley. It had to do with purity and fertility, rooted among the ancient pre-Hindu, pre-Buddhist religions of Asia. The living goddess was incarnated over and over. Similar to a woman playing different roles throughout the day, as housekeeper, mother, or lover, the goddess assumed many forms. She appeared as a virgin or a healer, as a mother or seductive goddess. When the girl who embodied Kumari experienced her first menses, the spirit passed to another. Local priests chose the new Kumari based on thirteen characteristics. She must be naturally beautiful and have the poise and dignity befitting a goddess. She must recognize certain personal items that belonged to the previous Kumari, like a comb or undergarment. These abilities were all recognized as signs of the goddess's incarnation.

"Hello? Miss! Hello! Hello!" It was a boy, about my age, dressed in gray slacks and a faded pullover. He grabbed my arm. "I, Rasua. I certified." Rasua handed me a card. The card said he was an English student at the local Tribhuvan University. "Will you be trekking?"

"I already have a guide." I pulled my arm from his grip.

He bobbed his head from side to side and grabbed my arm again. Taking several steps, he steered me from the palace. "I be your guide tonight. Tell me, where you from?" He smiled.

"America."

"Ah, yes, America. Very nice, very nice. Have you been to India?"

"Yes."

"Ah! India very poor. Some have . . ." He paused as if searching for the right words. "No things and some have much things. You see?"

I held back a smile.

"Here, not so. Everyone has a little. We happy. Come, come. I show you."

He pulled me down the steps. I followed, reluctantly. *How do I get rid of this guy?* A clatter of bells jangled in my ears, making me jump. I glanced up just in time. An angry rickshaw driver

shook his head as he swerved to miss us. My heart pounded; my
knees felt weak. Rasua appeared not to notice. He talked on and
on, pointing out various temples and statues. It was hard to follow
his choppy English. For a moment, I closed my eyes. The noise
and confusion were overwhelming. When I opened my eyes, I
noticed a crowd of agitated women elbowing each other. I paused.
What are they doing?

Rasua laughed. "Kumari Chowk."

"Kumari, what?"

"Chowk." He spoke slowly as if I were a child. "A king, Jaya,
very bad man . . ."

According to Rasua, the last Malla king committed an
atrocity when he raped a young Kumari. For his crime, he built
this temple.

"Why all the women?" I pointed at the crowd pressing
against the gate.

"Not allowed." Rasua shook his head. "Tonight is open, you
know . . ." He waved his hand. "But no women. Not for women."

"Why?"

Rasua ignored my question. "After three years, Kumari
spirit must pass to someone else." He flicked a fly away from his
face and turned to leave. I followed. "Kumari, our mother deity.
There are many, many gods in Nepal. But Kumari . . . Kumari is
people's god."

The people's god. It sounded like a political movement. How
could a young girl captivate so many people? Glancing around,
I felt as if I were looking through a kaleidoscope. I took in the
crowd, the odors, the crumbling buildings, and even a three-
legged dog. Maybe it was the jetlag, or not eating. Everything
felt unreal, like it was happening to someone else. Even my dirty
feet looked far away, as though they no longer belonged to me.

Reaching out to steady myself, I grabbed hold of a thin
metal bar. It felt cool against my skin. A cage. It was an iron

cage. Inside, a small black bear paced back and forth. His long, matted fur crawled with fleas. A tight-fitting muzzle clamped around his nose. Horrified, I stared. Why would anyone do this to a wild animal?

A group of boys with sticks sauntered toward the cage. They jeered at the creature and prodded him through the iron bars. The bear swung his head and stared at me with bloodshot eyes. Blood trickled from his nose. I wanted to shout at the boys to make them stop. I turned to Rasua. He was laughing.

I looked away. I felt sick.

Shadows now darkened the streets. It was getting late. People were leaving. The produce women had packed up their vegetables for the night. They glided away with their children in tow, balancing large baskets on their heads. Men chewing on beetle nuts lounged in doorways and spat in the streets.

Rasua put his arm around my shoulders. "Come, miss! My trekking shop, I show you!"

"No." I pulled away, shaking my head. "I'm tired. I need to sleep now." I rested my head against my hands and frowned. "I must go."

"Tomorrow?"

"Yes, yes, tomorrow." I nodded, backing away. He kept talking. I turned and hurried toward the nearest alley.

Alone, I took in a deep breath. The first stars appeared. A cool breeze filtered through the tepid alley. Something black fluttered above my head. Bats. I shivered. Where was my guesthouse? All the buildings looked the same. I stopped and glanced around. Nothing looked familiar. Panic ran up my spine. I trotted down one street, then another, then another. I was lost. My heart raced. I couldn't remember the direction from which I'd come. It was completely dark.

Suddenly, I heard a familiar sound: Bob Marley singing "Buffalo Soldier." A flashing neon sign announced the place: the

Blue Note Bar. I sighed. Now, I remembered. The Blue Note Bar was right next to my guesthouse. Warm yellow light spilled from the upstairs windows. Trekkers and tourists crowded together, drinking and laughing. I felt exhausted—and lonely. What was I doing here by myself?

Holding tightly to my keys, I unlocked the door. After climbing the stairs, I entered my room. Home at last.

As I slipped off to sleep, I kept seeing the tiny figure of the Kumari with her still, scared face—and those big, dark eyes. A crowd surrounded her. They chanted the same thing over and over. I didn't understand the words.

A few days later, I wandered back to the palace, hoping to catch a glimpse of the Kumari. I was curious about her. Did she want to be a Kumari? Did she miss her family? What would it be like to be worshiped as a deity?

The afternoon was gray and overcast. The last of the monsoon season seemed reluctant to leave. Bits of paper blew along the cobblestone street. Dogs lay sleeping in the alleys. After the wild exuberance of Indra Jatra, the city had settled back into itself. Horns beeped and bicycle rickshaws creaked through the narrow alleyways. Children dodged through traffic and tugged at my sleeves. Old women squatted along the sidewalk, selling herbs and spices. European tourists with beards and trekking poles drifted in and out of coffee shops. The city had a schizophrenic feel; wild and happy one moment, sullen and withdrawn the next.

According to my guidebook, foreigners were forbidden to visit the Kumari, but if you were lucky, she might make an appearance. Apparently, the girl liked to stand on the balcony of her third-story apartment and look down into the street. I read that her persona as a deity was orchestrated by the priests. Her exotic dress, makeup, even her presence and the way she carried herself, were staged to create a sense of mystery and otherworldliness.

I sat on the steps of the temple opposite Kumari Chowk and pulled out my notebook. As if on cue, a tiny form appeared behind the lattice. Dark eyes gazed down at me, unblinking. Her pale white face framed within the red and gold headdress reminded me of an exotic bird. The Kumari was not allowed to show emotion. She would not wave or smile or speak to a foreigner. I sat there as we stared at each other through the latticework. She struck me as curious and a little sad. I waved. Just a small gesture of acknowledgment. She gazed at me as if trying to figure out who I was and what I wanted. Large black eyes opened wide, and a slight nod tilted her face to one side. Did she actually notice me? Then, she was gone.

A raindrop landed on my arm. I glanced up. Brooding clouds swirled high above my head. Larger drops spattered onto the dusty streets. I shoved my journal into my bag and headed back to the guesthouse. Something about the image of a young girl dressed like a doll and held captive depressed me. I would be lonely if I had to play a role so carefully defined. Wouldn't she rather be running and playing like other children? My mood spiraled as I hurried past several men selling Tiger Balm. Beggars held out their hands, hoping for a few coins. Images of the Kumari kept flashing through my head. Like the afternoon at the temple in India, a quiet despair settled upon me.

Was I trapped too? If yes, then what was it? Had I grown up inside a role that didn't really fit me? Maybe it was the years of Sunday school and church services and missionary talks that made me feel caged. Was Kumari as powerless in her role as child goddess as I was growing up inside the tight embrace of my church?

By the time I dragged myself up the stairs of my room, exhaustion overwhelmed me. I lay on the gray mattress and watched the rain fall. What was I doing here? Had I changed from a few years ago? I really wasn't an anthropologist. What good had I accomplished? Was I just another tourist, collecting experiences to impress my family and friends?

My first few days in Kathmandu passed in a blur—the people, the rickshaws, the crumbling temples. I wandered through the city feeling alternately euphoric and homesick. I thought about the upcoming months. It was just the end of September, and I would be here until Christmas. My supervisor expected me to study different ethnic groups. Every night, I spread my ethnography books on the ragged mattress. My headlamp bobbed across the pages as I read about obscure people with complicated names that lived in remote valleys.

It sounded medieval. The two hundred ethnic groups of Nepal were scattered throughout the countryside. They lived in villages, miles away from the nearest road. They grew their own crops. They worshipped mysterious nature deities. They held festivals to guarantee a good harvest. Next door, the Blue Note Bar hummed with music. The occasional drunken brawl interrupted the otherwise quiet night. I read until I fell asleep.

The day before I left Kathmandu to trek, I visited Swayambhunath, a two-thousand-year-old pilgrimage site that overlooked the city. Everyone called it the Monkey Temple. To reach it, I had to climb three hundred sixty-five steps up a stone staircase. The staircase wound through a dark forest littered with Buddhas, prayer flags, and sacred shrines. According to tradition, the Monkey Temple spontaneously emerged from a lotus flower that bloomed out of a lake that once formed the Kathmandu Valley. Manjushri, the Bodhisattva of wisdom and learning, was raised on this hill. In rebellion, he grew his hair long. Lice collected on his magical hair, which eventually turned into the monkeys who live in the temple today. They are considered holy descendants of this magical transformation.

It was late afternoon. People streamed up and down the ancient staircase. Those going up stayed to the right; those going down, to the left. The haphazard steps were cut into the hillside. I watched my feet so as not to trip on an uneven stone. On either side of the staircase, large trees with smooth gray bark and pear-shaped leaves framed the way.

Midway up, I paused to catch my breath. Rain clouds rolled in, and a strong wind blew dust and grit into my eyes. From there, I could see the whole Kathmandu Valley. Rimmed by white-capped mountains, the city stretched out in a jumble of crumbling red buildings and zigzagging roads. On the outskirts, the buildings seemed to disappear into checkered fields of green and yellow. The recent rains had turned the valley a darker shade of green.

It took me almost an hour to reach the top. The stupa was surrounded by shrines, prayer wheels, and smaller temples. The courtyard crawled with tourists, beggars, and monkeys. Sadhus, Indian holy men, lounged around the temples. They wore bright-orange robes, and their faces were smeared with ash. Their matted dreadlocks grazed the ground.

"Hello? Hello?" They touched their fingers to their lips, nodding their heads to one side. "Money, miss. Hello?"

I leaned against a stone wall. There was so much to take in. A long time ago, the stupa must have been beautiful. Today, however, the whitewashed walls were stained brown with dust and filth. Great Buddha eyes peered from the gold-plated turret on top. The dank odor of urine hit me from an open doorway. I cringed. I would wait outside.

Monkeys ruled Swayambhunath. Tiny blond-haired babies clung to their mothers with anxious and unblinking eyes. Males with their bright-red faces and bushy eyebrows peered at me. A sign printed in English warned, "Danger: Do Not Look at Monkeys in the Eyes." Another sign said not to leave bags unattended. Everywhere I looked, monkeys were digging through tourist backpacks or swinging from the temple rooftop. Off to the side, several monkeys fought and leaped over each other, their long tails arching gracefully behind them. I jumped as a monkey fled past, clutching on to a camera.

"Hello, miss?" A slender man in flowing Punjabi pants and a white turban touched my arm.

"Hello." I pulled away, clutching my purse.

The man said something in Hindi that I couldn't understand. I shook my head.

He took my hand and turned it over, motioning with his finger. He was a palm reader.

"No, thank you." Feeling my cheeks flush, I sighed. I was tired of being hassled.

Again, the palm reader reached for my hand.

A tiny part of me was curious. *What would he say? Do I want to know my future?* In church, divination of any sort was considered demonic, the equivalent of voodoo or witchcraft. Even reading horoscopes was considered bad. Delving into the darkness could invite evil spirits. Luckily for me, I wasn't a Christian anymore. I was an anthropologist.

I nodded. Why not?

He motioned for me to sit.

I sat cross-legged on the ground, smoothing my skirt over my legs.

The palm reader squatted before me. His face bent over my outstretched hands. I bit my lip. His fingers, covered in rings, shook as his skin touched mine. Maybe he was nervous. Delicately, he traced the lines across my palm. He looked at me. I looked back. My heart pounded. Was he reading my palm or seeing into my thoughts? The man said nothing. His eyes shone brown with flecks of gold. He looked younger than I first thought. My palms grew sweaty.

"You have a good heart," he whispered. "You are a peaceful girl."

I smiled. It seemed like a compliment.

"You make up your mind to do things, and then you do them."

Yes, that was true.

The palm reader frowned. "You have a good heart. You are happy." He slapped his heart, looking frustrated, as though I did not understand his message. Was I not responding the right way? "You are independent and free right now." He leaned forward. "And, for always."

He looked at me as though he had pronounced something profound. When would he say something about my future?

At last, he sighed and shook his head. "You should not marry young. But when you do, you will have three great loves, all in one life. You have already known one of these loves. The second will come. And the third . . . he will be your husband." He smiled. "In the meantime, live and work. You will live in many different countries."

I smiled back at him.

"It is good, very good." He tapped his heart. "It will be okay. But . . ." He paused. "You must finish your studies." He nodded. "Do not quit your schooling. Study many different things."

"Okay." Did he know I fantasized about dropping out of school?

"Everything will be okay."

He looked at me again, this time with suddenly kind eyes. "You will be happy in your life."

It felt awkward. What was a person supposed to do when someone told them their destiny? *Should I just smile and say thank you? Should I cry? Maybe laugh?* Feeling silly, I wiped away a tear.

"A hundred rupees please." He held out his hand.

I pulled the bill from my wallet and handed it to him. He frowned and said something that, again, I didn't understand. He stared at me. Was he waiting for a tip? I hesitated. When he waved his hand, I stood up and walked away.

I never did find out what I had done to offend that man. Reading my future was probably a scam. It wouldn't be hard to decide that Western tourists were independent and lived long, happy lives. Statistically, having three great loves would be a good guess. Yet, I felt ridiculously happy, as though I'd been given a great gift—a gift of well-being. A promise that my life would be good. That I would have everything I wanted—love, travel, adventure, and fulfilling work. As I made my way down the staircase, the setting sun spilled bright rays through the clouds. I was happy. I was nineteen. The future stretched out before me, dark and mysterious and full of possibility.

CHAPTER THREE

◁⫶▢◉⫶▢◉⫶◉⫶◉⫶◉▢⫶◉▢⫶▷

MY TRIP TO THE Himalayas started when I visited my advisor
at Seattle Pacific University. I wanted to do an independent study
program. His office was a quiet, book-filled room on the third
floor of Arneson Hall. I paused in the open doorway. *Should
I knock?*

"Hello there." Dr. Tollefson swiveled around in his chair and
leaned back. His hands were crossed behind his head. "It's Julie,
right?"

"Yes."

Dark ritual masks hung above bulging bookcases and stacks
of papers. Beaded ceremonial headdresses and cloaks and
drums lay scattered across the room. They were all gifts from
West Coast tribes, which he had spent his life studying. One day,
I wanted to have an office like his.

"What can I do for you, Julie?"

Dr. Tollefson, a small man with soft black eyes and a pleasant,
almost timid demeanor, was the dean of the anthropology
department. Everyone loved him.

"I'm thinking about doing an independent study." I clutched
my backpack to my chest and breathed in the aroma of old wood

and peppermint tea. Outside, the rain had been coming down in sheets. Now, my soaked boots clung to my feet. I could feel water seeping past my toes.

"Have a seat." He gestured to a chair.

Perched on the edge of an overstuffed chair, I folded my hands together to hide their shaking. I was young, only eighteen. Would he agree to let me go abroad? Was I wasting his time?

"And where would you like to go?"

I knew where I wanted to go, but it was crazy. I wanted to go to the Himalayas. Himalayas, I said it over and over in my head as if it were a chant. Himalayas, Himalayas, Himalayas. Sitting in Dr. Tollefson's office, it sounded even more ridiculous. I wasn't a mountaineer or an adventurer. I had no money—no relatives with money, either. Somehow, the idea of the Himalayas had been growing in the back of my mind, ever since India.

In India, I had bought a map of Southeast Asia. I spent hours poring over the tiny squiggles of roads and dotted villages, trying to figure out where I was in the clutter of lines and dots. My gaze drifted up to the thin, rectangular country of Nepal. Tracing the blue contour lines, I wondered about the mountains. What did they look like in person? Nepal had fewer roads, fewer villages. Blue circles marked the glaciers and lakes. Suffering in the sultry heat of Southern India, Nepal seemed like a magical place, home to the highest mountains on earth. I imagined myself with a backpack, surrounded by peaks and meandering trails. What if I came back to Asia one day on my own? What if I wasn't with a missionary group? What if I was by myself? Could I travel alone as a girl?

"I want to go to the Himalayas," I said.

"Why the Himalayas? Why not somewhere closer to home?"

Most anthropology students chose independent studies on the Olympic Peninsula or reservations near Seattle—someplace where they might have friends or relatives.

I couldn't tell Dr. Tollefson that I wanted to go to the Himalayas because I had a fantasy of myself as a world traveler-backpacker. In my imagination, I was fit and confident, with bleached-out hair and a suntan.

In 1995, Nepal was a popular destination for people from Seattle. Import stores sold prayer flags, Buddha statues, handmade woolen hats, and Tibetan rugs. People in the stores wore baggy pants and Birkenstock sandals. They attended meditation classes. They spoke calmly. They seemed to be enlightened. Was that what I wanted? A new image of myself? Was I trying to recreate an awkward missionary girl and turn her into a savvy anthropologist?

The answer was *yes*.

Church had been part of my life for as long as I could remember. Growing up along the Columbia River in Washington State, my family attended the Church of the Nazarene, a sprawling, cedar-sided building just off the highway under a mountain called Castle Rock. It was built with hopes for a congregation of several hundred but never grew beyond more than fifty or sixty members at any one time. During services, we sat scattered throughout the echoing sanctuary.

In my family, church was not a place you just visited on Sundays. It was a way of existing. Weekly, monthly, and daily activities formed the fabric of our lives. It was a constant reminder of how things *ought to be*.

During Sunday school, we sat on metal folding chairs while cheerful ladies in long dresses with sweaters and big necklaces led us through a variety of children's songs. One of the songs required us to jump up when it was our turn. If we didn't leap to our feet fast enough, they'd make us do it all over again. And again. And again. There were songs with hand motions and lots of smiling. The teacher pointed to her cheeks and smiled really big. If we didn't smile big enough when it came to our turn, we had to stand up in front of the group and sing alone, smiling.

After the songs, which were supposed to excite us about Jesus, it was time for the lesson of the day. Usually the lessons were based on a Bible story, such as *Jonah and the Whale* or *Manna from Heaven*. The teacher read us the story and asked questions until we fully understood the message, which had to do with obedience to God and something called *evangelism*. The whale swallowed Jonah because he refused to go to Nineveh and tell the people the Good News. I wanted to obey Jesus, but spreading the Good News made me uncomfortable. I wondered about the people in Nineveh. What if they didn't want to hear the Good News?

At our house, my parents hosted Monday night Bible Study, which my sister and I liked. We crouched on the stairs to eavesdrop while the adults talked about serious things. Sometimes people cried. The crying piqued our curiosity because it meant that something was going on, something we weren't supposed to know about. We'd hold our breath and wait to sneak into the kitchen and steal some cake. Once, we heard that someone was getting a *divorce*. Another time, someone was having an *affair*. Sometimes people had a hard time.

It was important to my parents that I knew about God. Who God was. What He wanted for us and how to live in God's will. I was taught to honor my father and mother. Not to lie. Not to steal. Not to cheat. It was important to love my neighbor and to wear a dress. Act this way, not that way. Think like this. Believe like that. Become like this.

Even at the young age of eight, the messages blurred together. Over time, I couldn't separate what was the church and what was me. The multiweekly functions served as a framework, a close-knit web of familiarity. I knew we were supposed to feel a part of this community and a part of the church, as my parents did. We were supposed to enjoy the socializing, but to me it felt more like a prison. I wanted to love Jesus. I wanted to know God. But the taller I grew, the more something didn't fit. I felt fake. Especially there.

Once, when I was about six, our church hosted a revival meeting featuring a pastor from Atlanta. It lasted for three whole nights. The pastor's smooth black skin and rolling accent fascinated me. He wore a suit and tie and shiny black shoes. When he talked, he pointed his finger in the air and rocked back and forth on his heels. I'd never seen anyone like him before.

"Brothers and sisters in the Lord, how y'all doin'?" He smiled at us. The sanctuary was packed. People stirred the hot, stale air by waving programs in front of their faces. I smiled at the man. The worship band played a lively rendition of the "Saints Go Marching In." Everyone clapped and sang along.

Then the pastor launched into a story about his life. He had been a sinner and a drug addict. But God found him when he was at his lowest point in life. He was almost dead, and God rescued him. By the time he finished his story, everyone was wiping their eyes.

"Let me ask y'all something. How many of you are saved? Do you know if you're saved?"

I had been saved since before I could remember. My mother said I accepted Jesus into my heart when I was only two. But this night, I wondered if she was wrong. "Is your name written in the Book of Life?" The pastor held a Bible and pointed to the open page. "Can you tell me beyond a shadow of a doubt that you've been saved and redeemed by the blood of the lamb?" It was a chant: "Saved and redeemed, blood of the lamb." As if on cue, the tune "Washed by the Blood" played on the piano in soft, haunting tones.

"Do you hear Him?" The pastor wiped his brow with a white handkerchief. "He's knocking. Jesus is knocking at the door of your heart. Will you let Him in?"

I sat four rows back in a middle pew. My heart pounded. *Am I saved? How do I know for sure if I don't remember?* I grew up with the image of Jesus knocking at my heart. In my mind, he wore a long gray gown. His soft brown hair fell around his shoulders. He stood all alone in the dark, knocking on a little round door—the door to my heart. *What do I do?* All around me people were standing and running to the altar. Tears streamed down their faces as they fell to their knees. Was it wrong to get saved again? Would he know that I had already been saved? If I was saved once, was I saved for life?

I squeezed my eyes shut. When I opened them, my sister was gone. Where did she go? There she was, up front. I could see her purple striped blouse and her blond hair, touching the floor. If Jennifer was getting saved again, then maybe I should too. Heart racing, I stood. My palms were wet. The floor seemed very far away. As if in a dream, I stumbled to the front of the sanctuary.

"Thank you, Lord Jesus!" The black pastor shouted into the microphone. "Another one of your lost sheep has been found. Darling," he said as he knelt down until he was eye level with me, "did you feel the knocking?"

I nodded, hardly daring to look at him.

"Do you have any sins to confess?"

This part I had not thought about. I wanted to have a really good sin, but what? I was only six. My biggest problems were learning to read and worrying if my kittens would go to heaven with me. Sins were things like cheating in school. Or stealing gum. Or lying about eating the cookies.

Sins were also more complex. My mother used to sit next to me on the grass under our weeping willow. She told me about important things. We talked about my grandfather dying. We talked about my cousin, Sarah, who was severely disabled since birth. No one knew why, but we were all hoping for a miracle.

Suddenly, kneeling at the altar with tears running down my

cheeks, I remembered my secret sin: envy. I envied my sister and cousin Becky for their hair. Becky had shiny red pigtails that bounced when she ran. My sister had long white-blond hair that everyone admired. I had short dirty-blond hair that wasn't pretty. Sometimes people mistook me for a boy. Did this count as a sin?

"I wish I was pretty," I whispered. "I wish I had my sister's hair."

"What was that?" The big man leaned down.

I said it again, only a little louder. "I wish I had my sister's hair."

The big man shook his head. Either he didn't understand me, or there was no forgiveness for jealousy. He placed his right hand on my head and asked the Lord to come into my heart. Then he moved on to the next person.

I sat there, squeezing my eyes shut. *What should I do now? How long do I sit here?* I peeked at the people next to me. They were still praying and crying. Some smiled as though they were happier than they had ever been. I felt empty and strange. I knew I didn't belong there. My heart didn't feel any different. Had Jesus come into it like he was supposed to? Maybe I was too young for Jesus. Maybe he had more important people to save.

I sat there until my knees ached. I sat there until the service ended. I sat there until my mother came and put her arms around me. We rode home in our big brown car that smelled like vinyl. In the backseat, I looked at my sister. I wanted to ask her what happened to her at the altar. She wouldn't look at me. She just stared out the window. Everyone remained silent as we drove through the darkness.

I felt that way again, like I was a fraud with the missionaries in India. Every night during that long, hot summer, I prayed for a sign that I was supposed to be there. "Please God, send me a sign." Every morning when I woke up, I thought, *What am I doing here?*

On the front page of my journal, I copied a verse I had found before I left. It was Jeremiah 6:16. It read:

Stand at the crossroads and look;
ask for the ancient paths,
ask where the good way is and walk in it,
and you will find rest for your souls.

I loved this verse. In the church it was common to take verses out of context and apply them to your life. The Bible was like a good luck charm, full of mystical passages that could speak to you. The chapter from Jeremiah was all about war and the coming doom of Israel. It had nothing to do with travel or self-exploration, but I loved the way the words sounded. *The ancient paths . . . the good way . . . rest for your souls.* I repeated the verse from Jeremiah over and over until it became my mantra: *stand at the crossroads and look . . . ask where the good way is . . .*

Maybe the mountains would show me the way. Maybe I could find a different path. Maybe my path wasn't to be a missionary. Maybe it was something different altogether.

Sitting in front of the dean, two years after my first India trip, I felt as though I had found a new direction. "I want to study Tibetan Buddhism." My voice trembled. I cleared my throat. Would he say yes?

"Well," Dr. Tollefson said, eyebrows raised, "why don't you write up a research proposal? Submit it to me by the end of the month. We'll register you for a full independent study during fall term."

"So, is there a program, or a . . ." I wondered how to phrase what seemed like an obvious question. "Or an organization or something?"

Dr. Tollefson laughed. "No."

"So, I'll just go there and figure it out?"

"I imagine you'll do that."

On my way to class, I stopped in front of the clock tower. My thoughts raced. I was miserable. I hated living in the dorms. I hated the cafeteria food and the constant chatter of student life. The minute hand was just tipping to five after one. Late for class. I didn't care. I felt euphoric as though my life had just opened up. Now, all I had to do was step forward.

I spent the next six months reading about mountaineering and Tibetan Buddhism. I was excited to see the culture firsthand, but mostly I wanted to experience the Himalayas. That spring, I read a book about the first all-women ascent on Annapurna where one of the teammates died. Another had a love affair with a Sherpa porter. The harrowing descriptions of avalanches, crevasses, frostbite, and death entranced me. One night, I dreamed I was walking with my backpack along a trail with white mountaintops and deep gorges. The setting sun lit up the forest, and the trees glowed as if on fire. I would find the good way. I would find that ancient path. Maybe, just maybe, I would find peace.

CHAPTER FOUR

◁❙▢❂❙▢❙❂❙❂❙❂❙▢❙❂▢❙▷

AS THE LATE AFTERNOON sun descended behind the mountains, the bus shuddered around the final switchback and ground to a halt. I wiped a patch of dust from the window and peered out. Dark shadows hid the tall vertical ridges along the horizon. Glancing down, I stared into a narrow green valley. I took a deep breath and let it out slowly. I couldn't believe I was alive after that harrowing thirteen-hour ride, careening around hairpin turns and inching up steep cliffs.

"Holy crap, if that wasn't something." Kai, a thin, pale young man with acne scars and wild hair, unclenched his fists. He shifted in his seat and tried to stand, but the crush of people kept him folded in place. I glanced at him and frowned. Kai was a missionary. We were supposed to be traveling with a team of missionaries, but by some trick of fate we had been separated at the bus station this morning. When Kai and I had run ahead to catch the bus, the rest had lingered, bartering with a taxi driver for a better fair. They were left behind. Secretly, I was glad.

Would I ever be free of the missionaries? Earlier that summer, I agreed to stay with an American couple living in Kathmandu. Friends from our church suggested that I board with them. In their letter, they offered me room and board in exchange for me helping with their work. I had no idea where they lived, what they did, or what they would expect from me. I didn't want to stay with them. I wished I knew someone outside the church. But Christianity was like a spider's web. It stuck to me, shadowing my every move.

Louisa and Manek, the missionary couple, lived in an expatriate community called Jawalakhel. Their home was on the second floor of a two-story house. One floor down, an extended Nepalese family kept goats and a small vegetable garden in the backyard. In the mornings, I could hear the father downstairs clearing his throat and spitting. Often, the mother would yell at her kids. I'd hear the sound of a slap and then the sharp wail that echoed through the back room where I slept.

After a couple of days at my hosts' apartment, I thought I might go mad. The quiet place with its cross-stitched Bible verses and ticking clock made me want to scream. Outside, the city hummed with honking horns, barking dogs, and the roar of diesel engines. A new freeway was built just down the road. I felt trapped. At night, as I lay in the dark listening to the sounds of the city, waves of homesickness rolled over me. What was I doing there? How was I supposed to study different cultures from Kathmandu? I belonged in the mountains, not a bustling city. But where exactly would I go? How would I get there?

The next day, I borrowed Louisa's old 1950s bicycle and peddled to Thamel, the tourist district in Kathmandu. The morning sun shone above. A slight breeze blew against my face. I zigzagged down alleyways and main streets, swerving to miss the potholes. Men selling sweaters and roasted peanuts waved at me. Beggars with twisted limbs and cataract-glazed eyes shouted to get my attention, but I ignored them. A dog with a missing leg wandered the streets, and rickshaw drivers jangled their bells. I felt almost like a native.

After the hour-long ride, I stashed my bike and ordered a coffee at my favorite bakery. Munching a slightly doughy croissant, I sat near the window and watched tourists barter for goods. I wondered about Rasua, the guy who took me around on my first night in Kathmandu. Would he remember me? Was the Kumari girl still standing at the windows of her palace, trying to find me somewhere in the shadows?

Across the street, I noticed a man raising the window shades of a small bookstore. I swallowed the last of my coffee and wandered over. Breathing in the aroma of incense and books, I smiled. Bookstores always felt like home. They had a small section of books written in English. Even better, there were several recently published ethnographies on the different people of Nepal. Just what I needed. Thumbing through the pages, I studied the photos of people wearing traditional woolen dresses and shawls. They stood next to their mud homes, holding scythes as though they had just finished harvesting their fields. Forested slopes rose high behind them. White peaks loomed in the distance. The caption said that these were Jirels from Khumbu. Khumbu was near Everest. Mount Everest? Of course. That's where I wanted to go—Mount Everest.

That evening, I asked Louisa about the Jirels.

"You should talk to Anita." She sipped her tea and pushed her glasses up higher on her nose. Freckles stood out against her pale cheeks. "She and her sister lived with the Jirels for a long time. I believe they were the first foreigners in Jiri. They even started a school. You should probably make plans to meet her."

"Really?"

"Yes, her sister died a couple years ago, but Anita still lives in Kathmandu. I have her number somewhere."

Louisa left to find the phone number. I sat there, fidgeting in the seat. Did she assume I planned to convert the Jirels? Not once since I arrived had the issue of my faith, or lack of it, come up. Was the silence intentional? Louisa was young, only a couple of years older than me. Her parents were postal workers in Michigan. She had only lived in Nepal for a few months with her new husband, Manek. He was from the Philippines. My presence was probably as difficult for them as their neat little home felt to me. We had nothing in common. She'd never been to college. She didn't like trekking or recreating in the mountains. *How strange,* I thought. *Living in Nepal and not visiting the mountains.*

Yet, her steely determination to learn the language impressed me. Every day, she took Manek's moped to a nearby language school. She practiced her Nepali while buying groceries and running errands. Every night, she cooked old-fashioned Midwestern meals such as hamburger casseroles and baked puddings. Sometimes when I arrived home unexpectedly, I heard her crying in the bedroom. Later, she emerged smiling, her eyes reddened and swollen. Louisa was just twenty-one.

A few days later, I climbed the staircase of the old Summit Hotel in Jawalekhel to meet Anita, the mysterious German missionary. She had refused to talk over the telephone, insisting that we speak in person. Stepping onto the rooftop, I glanced around. Rain clouds clung to the surrounding mountains, and a stiff breeze rattled my notebook pages. Green fields dotted with red brick buildings and white cows stretched out for miles. The German woman was small. Smaller than I imagined. She wore her white hair tucked into a neat bun. Her floral dress flowed down to her leather clogs. She did not return my smile.

"Who you are?" she whispered in a thick German accent. "What is it you want?"

"I'm Julie. We spoke on the phone. I'm the anthropology student."

"American?"

"Yes."

"How did you find me?"

"Louisa." My heart raced. Clearly this was not going well. I wasn't sure if it was because I was American or an anthropologist. "I want to know about the Jirels."

She pursed her lips and glanced around. We were alone on the rooftop, except for a young man from the hotel watering red geraniums in terracotta pots. She waited until he left.

"Okay, we can talk."

"Louisa told me that you and your sister began the first school in Jiri." I hoped she would warm up and chat naturally.

"We did."

"What was that like?"

"It took years." Anita glared at me. "Listen, what do you really want?"

"Uh..." I searched for a better question. "What do the Jirels believe in?"

"They are animists. They believe in nature spirits." Anita pulled her brown shawl tightly over her shoulders.

"I see." But I didn't see. I wanted to know what it was like for her to come to Nepal as a young girl in the 1950s. What was it like to live in a remote village long before telephones or even roads? Louisa said Anita and her sister had come to Nepal before the country was open to foreigners. What was Nepal like back then? Why would two sisters come all the way from Germany to translate the Bible into the Jirel language? What were animists? What was a nature spirit? How did you worship one?

But Anita was cold and agitated, answering my questions in monosyllables.

"How long did it take you to learn the language?"

"Two years."

"Louisa said you translated part of the New Testament to Jirel?"

"Yes."

"And what else did you do?"

"We started a health clinic."

"By yourself?"

"With a doctor from England, yes."

"Wow. That's amazing." I didn't know what to say. Later, I learned that before the Democratic Party took over in 1990, Christianity was illegal in Nepal. Even now, in 1996, it was illegal to convert someone from the religion of their birth. Proselytizing was against the law, and rumors circulated among the Christian community that converts were thrown in jail.

"Did you convert a lot of people?"

"Some." Anita looked out at the horizon and frowned. "I met an anthropologist once. He was a very silly man. He didn't last long." She gathered her purse and moved toward the stairs.

I followed her, shivering in the cold breeze that suddenly scattered the marigold petals across the rooftop.

"In the old days," Anita said, "you never knew who you could talk to. You couldn't trust anyone."

"I want to visit the Jirels."

"That's great." Louisa stared out the window. "Maybe the Colorado team could go with you." She turned, suddenly eager. "They're coming here next week! Maybe you could talk to them and you could all go together."

I must have looked reluctant because she hurried on. "I don't have time to work with them, and Manek has to be at the fish farm. But you could. They could help you with your fieldwork, interviews, or whatever." She smiled, pleased.

My heart sank. Now, I would be stuck with yet another missionary team tramping around the mountains, trying to do fieldwork. Why had I even said anything to her? Why hadn't I just left?

I met the missionaries from Colorado three days before our departure to Solu Khumbu. As I strolled the few blocks to their hotel, the setting sun cast an orange glow over the brick buildings. I hummed, happy that I had organized the trekking permits and figured out the bus schedule. In a few days, I'd be out of the city for at least three weeks.

Knocking lightly on the half-open door, I peered into a large room with three or four twin beds. Ancient green carpets covered the floor. Heavy drapes shaded a small window. On one of the beds sat a girl with pale skin and long dark hair. She held a hairbrush and clenched bobby pins between her lips. Another girl with short red curls and large-framed glasses sprawled out next to her, reading a Bible.

"Hello?" I peeked around the door and smiled.

A woman rummaging through a backpack glanced up at me. She frowned. She was probably in her mid-thirties, slightly overweight with brown hair and stern lips. She gave me a brief nod. "I'm Charla."

"I'm Julie." I stepped into the room.

"Does anyone have more shampoo?" Charla held up an empty travel container. The girls shook their heads.

My palms started to sweat. Why were they ignoring me? I cleared my throat. "You like Nepal?"

"We're all tired." Charla spoke for the group.

The girls studied me warily. Charla knew I was an anthropologist. Louisa told me she had spoken to her earlier. Did they know what an anthropologist was? I smoothed my hair and laughed nervously. The red-haired girl muttered something before turning back to her Bible. The girl with the brush glanced down at her lap.

"Perhaps I should just wait downstairs." I backed out of the room, my heart sinking.

What is it with these people? How will I ever endure three weeks in the mountains with them?

An hour later, we met for dinner on the rooftop. Strings of tiny white lights lit the red checkered tablecloths. Hindi pop music blared from cheap speakers. It looked like we were the only guests tonight. I glanced down the table. Two young men sat by Charla. A couple of girls I hadn't met yet just arrived. The dark-haired girl sat next to me, fingering the tablecloth. No one spoke.

"So, why did you choose Nepal?" I asked, trying to make conversation.

"I didn't." The dark-haired girl took a sip from her Nalgene bottle. "My heart's in Israel, but I guess God had other plans for me."

"Israel?" I said.

"Yes, I spent last summer working at a church in the West Bank."

"Then, why Nepal?"

"God called me."

I tried not to roll my eyes. It wasn't that I didn't understand the jargon, I did. Just two years ago, I might have said that God called me to India. But I would have been wrong. I was starting to see that now.

The red-haired girl leaned across the table. "God called *me* to drop out of medical school."

I stared at her. *She dropped out of college?* "How do you know that God wanted you to do that?"

She frowned.

"What I meant was, how could you *tell* that God wanted you to drop out of school?"

"I just knew." The red-haired girl shook her head and sighed as though it was obvious. God talked to everyone that way. Right? Everyone but me.

Walking home in the dark, my mind churned. These missionaries were so sure of themselves. One even dropped out of medical school. How could that possibly be God's will?

Above my head, insects whined around bright streetlamps. A rickshaw wheeled slowly past. I had always tried to hear God's voice. In Sunday school, we read the story of God speaking to Moses through the burning bush. I never expected to experience anything that dramatic, but I always tried to hear the still, small voice. In high school, I even took classes on discerning God's will. Again, I never felt it. Had God ever talked to me?

At the corner near my duplex sat at a small Hindu shrine. It wasn't much bigger than a phone booth. Inside, a woman and two small boys lit a candle. The flame sputtered in the darkness. For a moment, their faces reflected the warm glow. They knelt and rubbed vermilion on the god's head. Then all three bent their heads in prayer.

Standing there, I thought about the missionaries. They would see this deity and the woman with her boys as demonic. They would pray for her. They might even intervene and try to stop her. Ultimately, they would see dysfunction and darkness where I was beginning to see poverty and magic. The missionaries believed that God watched over them. They believed that everyone else was lost. If they were here right now, they would say that God had led them to be here on this dark street corner at this time. Well, maybe the missionaries were right. Maybe I was supposed to be here, right now. Maybe I could hear God's voice. Maybe I was supposed to see that God watched over all of us, in all our different faiths. Maybe this was my calling.

That was four days ago. Now, I was waiting to get off a bus with Kai. We'd left the rest of the missionary group behind. My legs ached from sitting thirteen hours on a hard seat. My dress clung to my skin. Standing, I grabbed my pack and stumbled after Kai. Outside, a warm breeze carried the scent of pine and juniper trees. Faintly, I could hear water rushing from somewhere in the valley below.

Kai and I looked around. A single main street bisected the town, lined on either side with lodges and fabric shops. Two pigs picked their way through piles of litter scattered along the road. Chickens scratched in the dirt. Stagnant water lay puddled in the street.

"Let's find a guesthouse." I sniffed—cooked rice and campfire smoke. I glanced toward the row of guesthouses. They all looked the same—dark, dirty, and empty.

"We should call Charla," Kai reminded me for the umpteenth time. "I have to tell her what happened."

"Mmm." I smiled, pleased to have lost the group so soon. Any day without them was a relief. "Let's get a room and ditch our packs first."

Tiptoeing through the mud, we made our way toward the Yeti Hotel, a tall building with blue trim and whitewashed walls. The front door stood ajar.

"Hello?" We stepped inside. Fire crackled from a dome-shaped mud oven. The room was dark and smelled like old wood and dust. A thin young man with a sparse mustache sat hunched before the fire, stoking the coals with a stick. He cleared his throat and spat into the flames.

"Do you have a room?"

The man did not answer. He motioned for us to follow him. We tiptoed up a narrow staircase and stopped at the first door. He gave it a push. We peeked inside. The room was bare except for two twin mattresses. A low window faced the street.

"How much?" I asked.

"Twenty rupees."

I let my pack slide to the floor. "Is there a shower?" I showed the man my bar of soap. "Shower?"

"Yessss." He drew his s's out, motioning for me to follow him again. Behind the building sat a dark little shack. A hand pump was just off to one side.

"Thank you." A shower was my first priority.

"Phone?" Kai asked.

"No phone." The man shook his head and turned away. His shuffling steps echoed down the dark hallway.

Kai sighed. "I have to find a phone."

"Let's go back to the bus station and see if they have one there." My shower would have to wait.

I stood outside while Kai tried to communicate with the station master. Through the dusty window, I watched as he made exaggerated gestures of holding a telephone to his ear. I stifled a laugh.

Gazing at the valley below, I sighed. The team from Colorado was with an organization called YWAM, or Youth with a Mission. Like Teen Missions in India, YWAM took teens from all over the United States and trained them in Bible Study and evangelism. Then they sent them on trips around the world to do service projects and convert people to Christ. YWAMers, as we called them, were a little looser and genial than my teammates from India but just as evangelically minded. I was embarrassed to be associated with them.

"They're coming the day after tomorrow," Kai said, rejoining me outside. Apparently, tomorrow was a national holiday. So, no buses. His cheeks were flush. Had Charla chastised him for leaving them behind? You could be expelled or sent home for something like that.

Later, over a meal of rice and lentils, we met a handful of trekkers leaving for Everest in the morning. They had long sun-bleached hair and beards. They wore prayer beads and hemp bracelets. They just came from Thailand and India. Nepal was the next stop on the Asian circuit.

Pulling apart some hot chapati bread, I listened to their conversations.

"Khoa San Road is crazy, mate," one man said.

Another shook his head. "Yeah, did you stay at the Yard?"

They all laughed.

"How about Goa?" another asked.

"Oh my god . . . the night I spent there."

I kept quiet and hoped Kai would too. I didn't want anyone to know that Kai was a missionary.

One of the guys ordered a round of beers. "You want one?" He smiled at me.

"No, thanks. I'm okay." I fiddled with my water bottle.

Kai struck up a conversation with a guy about camera brands. They were discussing the new Nikon F2. "I think the lens is better on the F100."

"No, really?"

"Yeah, I read this review . . ."

The rest of the guys moved on to drinking stories.

I stifled a yawn and glanced around the dimly lit dining hall. Three rectangular tables sat empty. Did the place fill up during the main trekking season, or was it always this empty? I tapped my fingers on the table, absently. Maybe I should head back to the room.

A small boy with a wide lopsided grin arrived with six beers teetering dangerously on a metal tray. I held my breath. The bottles slid as he bent awkwardly toward the table.

I jumped up to help him. "Here."

"Thank you, *didi*." The boy beamed at me. He was short and slight. I guessed he was around twelve. His dark eyes sparkled.

I smiled. *Didi* is a term used for an older sister. I liked that he called me that.

"What's your name?" I asked.

"Jimmy." His voice sounded hoarse and gravelly.

"You work here?"

He ducked shyly and scuffed his bare foot against the floor. He hurried out, returning almost immediately with a stout, jolly man.

"Excuse me, miss . . . you have something to say?"

"Oh, not really." My cheeks flushed. "I was just asking if he worked here."

"Ah yes, Jimmy is hard worker." He patted the boy affectionately on the head.

"You speak English?" I asked.

"A little."

"Do you know any Jirels in the area?"

"Yes, yes. Jimmy is a Jirel." The jolly man lowered his voice and whispered, "But Jirel people—they are no good. Very poor, very dirty. No education." Brightening, he added in a loud voice as he prodded the boy's shoulder, "Jimmy here, he is a good Jirel!"

Because tomorrow was a holiday, Jimmy would go home to his village, an hour's walk from here.

"Can we go with you?" I asked impulsively. "Can I meet your family? For interviews?" Jimmy looked at the stout man, then back at me. He nodded, hesitantly.

"We meet here . . . tomorrow morning? Can you tell him that?" I asked the man.

"Yes, *didi*. Is no problem," the man replied. "Tomorrow morning, you go."

"There," I said to Kai as we made our way back to our room. "Now we have something to do tomorrow before Charla and the others come."

Kai shrugged. "If Charla finds out we're sleeping in the same room—"

"Get your own room!" I wished he would. But Charla had kept his money. He barely had enough to cover his dinner and half of our room.

He shook his head. "Just don't tell her. My parents will kill me if I get kicked out."

Over bowls of lumpy oatmeal, Kai and I watched the trekkers from last night fiddle with their packs. One of the guys filtered water from the stock tank. Another applied sunscreen after adjusting his trekking poles. Laughter filled the courtyard. I wanted to go with them. They looked like fun people. Jimmy stood in the courtyard, hopping from one foot to the other. He smiled and waved. I sipped my hot, sweet chai.

"Have a good one!" the guy with the sunscreen called out.

"Yep." I waved back. *Why can't I just be a normal person, traveling with guys like them?*

The trekkers drifted off, their voices floating behind in the still morning air. Reluctantly, I finished my oatmeal and laced up my boots.

"Okay?" Jimmy said.

A young man wearing a blue baseball cap and green trekking pants casually stubbed out a cigarette with his bare toe. He stood. "I come too."

I recognized him from last night in the kitchen. "I'm Julie." I hoisted my pack a little higher on my hip and smiled.

"Dawa," he bowed his head.

"Nice to meet you, Dawa. English?"

"Yes, madam." He grinned. "I speak English."

"Wonderful." I wasn't sure if he was accompanying us for Jimmy's benefit, or for ours, but I was glad to have an interpreter.

The sun shone bright and hot in the clear blue sky. Birds sang in the distance. Jimmy made a beeline toward the southern edge of town before plunging down a steep trail. I struggled to keep up with his short, fast stride. His little head bobbed up and down as he swung a plastic bag with something heavy in his right hand. We slipped into a single file with Jimmy in the lead, me close behind, then Dawa and Kai. The trail made several narrow switchbacks through a forest of tall evergreens. I breathed in the clean, tangy scent of juniper and fir. Rushing water echoed through the valley from somewhere below. The forest was cool and dark. Finally, I was doing real fieldwork. I couldn't believe that I'd managed to meet a Jirel during the first night in town. What was his family like? Would they speak English? Did they know we were coming? What should I ask them?

After an hour or so of walking, the trail leveled out. Through the trees, I glimpsed the sparkling Sikri River, which I had seen from above the night before.

"Market!" Dawa pointed toward the river. A large crowd of people gathered around saris piled high with vegetables, rice, and strange fruits I'd never seen. Men selling chai and little fried balls of dough circled through the crowd. Women hawked plump mangos and yellow bananas. My stomach rumbled at the scent of cardamom and cloves. I wanted to try one of the little dough balls, but a pack of barefoot children intercepted me.

"Pens! Pens, please!" They grabbed my hands and pulled on my skirt.

"No pens!" I shook my head and kept walking. They swarmed around me, laughing. "Pens, pens!" They clung to my legs. I couldn't move. Helplessly, I looked around. Where was Jimmy?

Jimmy strode ahead, waving proudly to the people he knew. The market had a festive air. Women with kohl-lined eyes balanced baskets on their heads. Babies gurgled on their hips. They talked fast, bartering for soap and household goods. Some had large lumps on their necks; goiters caused by iodine deficiency. *They must be poor. Do tourists come here from Jiri? How do they make a living?*

I glanced at Kai. The children had accosted him too. "No pens." He shook them off. He looked irritated. "Dawa!"

"*Tadha jane!* Go away!" Dawa shook his head. "Trekkers used to give out pens to the children. Very bad habit," he said. "No pens!" He yelled at the children. "Go!"

Together, we hurried past the market. The noisy din of people, chickens, and goats grew fainter as we trudged on.

The trail wound straight up the mountainside. My boots chafed at my heels. Sweat trickled down my back. The path, perhaps once wide and well packed, was now only a thin cat-track. Even Jimmy seemed to have trouble locating it. I looked around, panting. The relentless grind kept me tilted forward and my gaze fixed on the ground. Out of the corner of my eye, I noticed that we walked through what seemed like private backyards. We skirted vegetable gardens, terraced fields, and red-clay houses with thatched roofs. I would never have found my way alone. Children, hurrying down, stopped to stare at us, their brown eyes wide with curiosity.

"Pens, please?" one child said.

Pausing, I wiped the sweat from my forehead with the hem of my red dress. When would we get to the top? Why hadn't I stayed in town? I imagined sitting at the guesthouse reading and writing in my journal. What I wouldn't give for a strong cup of coffee and a bakery pastry. Pastries—what a nice thought. *What kind of pastry do I want? Chocolate éclair? Almond-filled croissant? Those little eggy-things I had a few weeks ago?* The thought of pastries happily occupied my mind for several more terraces. At last, the trail leveled out. I found myself on a high grassy plateau with tall fir trees.

I stopped to catch my breath. Ahead, Jimmy waited with his hands on his hips. A breeze stirred the trees. Bees buzzed in the grass. I licked my dry lips and unscrewed my Nalgene bottle. Dawa and Kai arrived, panting, behind me. We rested for a moment, looking around. In the middle of the grove sat an enormous rock smeared with red vermilion and draped with flowers. Around it, a circle of sticks had been dug into the ground. At the end of each stick, a strip of white cloth fluttered in the breeze.

"What is it, Dawa?" I felt like I should whisper.

Dawa turned to Jimmy. "It is a Kuladevata, their clan deity. There are twelve clans in this area. This is Jimmy's clan. They worship here during the full moon."

Jimmy stopped to bow before the stone. Kneeling, he placed his forehead to the ground.

The rest of us stood quietly, waiting. After several prostrations, Jimmy rejoined us. He said something to Dawa.

"It's a big party," Dawa said. "Dancing. Rice wine. All the family come together."

Beside me, Kai stood stiff and straight. His lips were pursed. Talk of deities and clans reinforced what the missionaries already believed about the Jirel. Now, he had proof that they were animists and needed Christianity. From my readings, I knew that while the Jirel observed many Hindu festivals, they also practiced Lamaistic Buddhism, a Buddhism based on their traditional animistic beliefs. A priest, or *phompo*, conducted worship here in this sacred grove. I gazed out over the expanse. Harsh sunlight shone in the valley below. Up here, however, the shade felt cool. All was quiet.

I wanted to ask more, but Jimmy turned to go. I took a gulp from my water bottle and followed him out of the forest and up the mountainside. At the next terraced slope, two small girls, wearing ragged dresses with wild, dark hair, appeared as if out of nowhere. They threw their thin arms around Jimmy's waist, laughing excitedly. He pulled away and ducked his head. Was he embarrassed? When the girls saw me and Kai, they stopped. Their eyes were wide. Maybe they never saw a white person before. Maybe they wondered what two strangers were doing at their home. Maybe we shouldn't have come.

Jimmy waved us to follow him into the family compound. "Come, come!"

An older man with white hair sat out front working with a narrow butter churn. He wore striped, tapered pants with a traditional waistband, called a *doura*, and a gray overcoat, or *lukini*, with a *khukuri* knife tucked into the waist. Unlike the girls, our appearance didn't seem to faze him. His weathered face creased with wrinkles when he smiled. Did he know we were coming? Jimmy turned toward the house where a small woman with bare feet and loose graying hair smiled shyly in the doorway.

The house was perched on a flat ledge high above the valley floor. Its mud walls were whitewashed at the base, leaving the top colored red with a mixture of dung and clay. From outside, the two-story house looked spacious and neat. As I bent under the low door frame, I caught my breath. The packed dirt floor was empty except for a few sleeping pads rolled up in a corner. A fire smoldered in the middle of the room. Blue smoke hung thickly in the air. My eyes watered.

"Namaste," I said, squatting across from Jimmy's mother.

She sat on her haunches, stirring the coals. Water bubbled in a blackened pot. I watched her toss a handful of dark tea leaves into the water. She glanced at me through the smoke. We smiled, cautiously, at each other, but said nothing.

The girls retreated to the second-floor loft. Lying on their bellies, they peered over the edge. I wished I knew their language. I wanted to talk to them. I felt out of place with my white skin and trekking boots. The mother poured tea into six small metal cups. Placing the cups on a tray, she walked outside, where the old man sat puffing on a fat cigar. Jimmy and Dawa squatted on either side of him. Kai sat cross-legged in the dirt. After helping the mother pass out tea, I sat beside Kai. We sipped our tea silently.

Next to the house sat a small vegetable garden with ripe golden-green soybeans. Cornstalks, already harvested, leaned against a pole to dry. Chickens scratched at the dirt. Jimmy's father sat, smoking contentedly. He seemed to have no need to make conversation or interact with us. The sun beat down, hot against my skin. A slight breeze stirred my hair.

After what seemed like a long time, a young man came laboring up the trail. He had smooth brown skin and dark hair. I couldn't guess his age, but like Jimmy, he wore new tennis shoes and a red baseball cap with a mountaineering insignia. The old man leaped to his feet, clasping the boy's hands.

"This is Sela—Jimmy's older brother," Dawa said as they greeted each other. "He's home for the holidays."

"What kind of work does he do?" I asked.

"He is a porter. He carries gear for tourists." Dawa gestured to the peaks in the distance.

"Which peaks do you climb?" I asked Sela.

"Ahh . . ." He squinted into the sun, pointing to two white peaks just visible along the horizon. "Sur," he said the name slowly and added, "Gaurishankar."

"Gaurishankar?" I repeated. According to my map, the peak was over seven thousand meters high. Gazing at the mountain, I shivered. What would it be like to climb a mountain that high? "How many people have climbed Gaurishankar?"

"Only a few. Maybe one, maybe two." Sela shook his head. "The mountain will not let them."

"There are many, many accidents," Dawa chimed in cheerfully. "All dead."

"All dead?" I stared at him.

"Yes." He clicked his tongue. "So many accidents. Everybody dies."

Later, I read that because Gaurishankar was so hard to summit, it had been closed to climbers for over twenty years. Many foreigners had died trying to climb it. Sitting there in the sun, I thought about climbing mountains. I remembered my books on the Annapurna. I thought about the stories of ice crevasses, avalanches, and altitude sickness. It sounded dangerous, but also . . . attractive. Would I climb mountains someday? I hoped so.

The mother appeared with another tray of spicy milk tea, soybeans, boiled eggs, and salt. Should Kai and I refuse the eggs? Were we eating the family's only source of protein? I glanced toward the house. Jimmy's sisters watched us from an upstairs window.

I leaned over to Dawa. "Do they want to eat?"

"No, no." He pushed the tray toward me. "Eat."

We sat in the sun for hours, smiling at each other and talking sporadically through Dawa and Jimmy's brother. The old man drank *chyang*, a homebrewed barley-beer. He drank glass after glass, growing more animated as the sun traversed the cerulean sky. The mother sat inside by the fire, smoking her pipe and muttering to herself. We asked if she might join us, but she never did. The little girls peeped at us through the upstairs windows. They would not emerge until we said our goodbyes and began the trek down the mountain.

That evening, I poured over my map. According to my book, Jirels lived between here and Ringmo, a village about a five-day-walk from here. The guesthouse owners, however, insisted that Jirels lived only here and in the surrounding valley.

"You must go to Bhandar, Junbesi, Lukla, Everest!" they said.

Weighing our options, I decided to trek at least as far as Ringmo, which looked like a Jirel village on the map. I could spend more time interviewing Jirels. Deep down, I didn't really care if I found more Jirels or not. I just wanted to keep hiking in the mountains. I wanted to trek as far as the Everest Base Camp. If only I didn't have the missionaries with me.

Later, I lay in my sleeping bag listening to dogs bark throughout the village. I wondered about Jimmy's little sisters. Would they ever learn to read, or would they work at a guesthouse like their brothers? Probably neither. Without books or television, what did they know about the world? In my mind, I kept seeing their dark eyes and wild hair and thin legs. What was their life like—full moons, magic, dances, boys, a harvest? A tiny part of me envied them. It would be a hard life, yes, but simpler. Maybe they didn't wonder about their place in the world like I did. Maybe they just accepted their lives.

The next morning dawned bright and clear. Snowy peaks abounded in every direction. I couldn't wait to get on the trail.

"Better check the bus station," I told Kai, stuffing my sleeping bag into its sack. The Colorado team was supposed to have arrived earlier this morning.

A few minutes later, Kai returned, fuming. "She's sick."

"Who's sick?"

"Charla."

"So?"

"So, they're not coming." Kai tossed a water bottle into his pack.

"What do you mean *they're not coming?*"

"I don't know—that's what they said. Charla's sick and they're not coming, and I have to take the first bus back this morning." He shoved things into his pack: toothbrush, iodine tablets, and dirty socks.

I stood there, considering my options. I hadn't relished the thought of spending three weeks with the missionary group. Kai was getting on my nerves with his fretting and worrying.

"Did Charla mention me?"

"No."

"She didn't ask what I was going to do?"

"No."

"Huh." Excitement surged in my stomach. "Well, I might go on."

"You can't." Kai stared at his pack.

"Why not?"

"It's not safe. You're a girl."

"I'll be fine."

I was a bit surprised—and hurt—that the missionaries didn't care about my safety. They must be more worried about what kind of influence I was on Kai. This only strengthened my resolve. I would continue by myself.

We said our goodbyes after a cup of milk tea and Power Bars. I left Kai looking gloomy at the bus station. A few yards up the trail, I glanced back. He shook his head. I grinned and waved. The day was impossibly clear. I wore an old cotton dress that I could wash every night and hang dry. I also wore hiking boots, a sweater, and prayer beads. At last, I was off. My first solo expedition in the mountains, six thousand miles from home.

Years later, I would remember that early morning with the sun on my face, the mountains stretching across the horizon, and the aroma of cooking fires. It was 1996. There were no cell phones or Internet access. I had last spoken to my parents from a payphone in Kathmandu three weeks earlier. It would be weeks before I would speak to them again. Had they missed me? Would they know where I was?

Standing on the trail that morning, I felt free. Everything in my past was behind me. The mountains beckoned. The birds sang. I felt like I was walking into my destiny. Every step took me farther along the path that I had to go.

CHAPTER FIVE

◁❏◉❶❏❶◉❶◉❶◉❶❏❶◉❏❶▷

IN ANCIENT TIMES, MOUNTAIN gods lived on the snowy peaks of the Himalayas. Each year as the snows receded, villagers planted their gardens, waited for the summer rains, and grazed their yaks in the alpine pastures. People depended on the mountains for their survival. Over time and through many generations, the mountains awoke, taking on distinctive personalities. In the isolated valleys, stories arose about what the mountains liked or disliked. Tales of disaster and miracles were told and retold. Rites and rituals shaped the landscape and enhanced the spirit of the mountains.

Here in Khumbu, Miyolangsangma, the mother goddess of Mount Everest was one of five demoness-sisters who settled on various peaks. The sisters wreaked havoc on local people. They caused mishaps, avalanches, and accidental deaths. According to legend, when he came to Tibet, the Buddhist master Padmasambhava converted the demonesses into protector goddesses. Once tamed, the sisters provided spiritual and physical nourishment to Khumbu and the surrounding valleys. In dark temples, Miyolangsangma was portrayed as a woman astride a female tiger. In her left hand she held a bowl of divine food, and in her right a lotus blossom.

The landscape teemed with spirits. The spirits lived on high passes, in waterfalls, and among sacred groves. Villagers wore protective amulets around their necks. At certain sites along the trail, they offered sacrifices. A high-pitched shriek at the top of each pass warned the gods of a traveler's presence and kept the spirits at bay.

As I trudged up the steep trail, no mountain god or evil spirit clouded the crystalline-blue sky. The air felt warm and dry against my cheeks. The morning breeze carried the lemony-scent of fir trees and wet earth. My heart thudded more from the adventure of starting off on my own than from the steep climb. At the top of the first pass, I paused. Scattered across the valley below, small farms and clay houses with thatched roofs dotted the landscape. I could see tiny gardens with bright-yellow flowers. Yaks grazed peacefully nearby. The slim outline of the Khimti River glittered in the sun.

Mountain gods fascinated me—they sounded like a fairy tale. I thought about the differences between the Himalayas and the mountains back home. In Washington, people considered wilderness a separate space, a place to visit. I went to the mountains to get away from people, away from society. Here, people were a part of the landscape. They didn't seek out an empty wilderness. It terrified them. Virgin forests and high mountain peaks were home to evil spirits. Never would the villagers consider the wild to be a place of peace or tranquility.

Glancing at the map, it looked as if I would spend the night in a village named Bhandar. To reach it, I had to cross the Khimti River and climb the 10,700-foot Deurali Pass. Deciphering a map by myself was exciting and frightening. I'd never backpacked alone, overnight. Would I find my way to the next village?

The day was hot by the time I reached the river. After a brutal toe-smashing descent through thick vegetation, I was dying of thirst. Empty water bottles dangled from my pack. Sweat soaked the back of my dress. Fumbling with the buckles, I let my pack fall to the rocks. Without the additional weight, I almost fell over. Grabbing the water purifier from the top of my pack, I stumbled to the water's edge. An icy breeze cooled my face. The sand around my boots glimmered with a gray, sparkly mineral. I filled my bottles. Sitting against the rocks, I guzzled greedily. The water was icy cold. It tasted like I was drinking from the belly of the mountain.

Satiated at last, I looked around. The river plunged down the narrow valley over boulders and gigantic slabs of rock. A metal suspension bridge hung high above the rapids. It swayed slightly in the breeze. On the opposite bank, a fisherman stood on a large rock. He bent over the water, a spear in his hand. I watched. His bare chest glistened in the sunlight. Something about him made me nervous. I wondered if I was allowed to be here. *Do people swim in this river? Is it considered sacred?*

It looked tempting. Dust covered my legs and arms. I needed a bath. I unlaced my boots and peeled off my grimy socks. Sharp rocks dug into my bare feet. Gingerly, I stepped into the water. I gasped as the cold water touched my skin. I took another step. The current swirled around my knees. I glanced at the fisherman. Did he care? He seemed not to notice me. I looked up at the sky—blue, impossibly blue. Steep green hillsides surrounded me. Sunlight danced on the water. I closed my eyes. I smiled. Joy. Pure, unadulterated joy. This was living. This was what I'd longed for.

I splashed water over my arms, face, and head. When my feet numbed, I staggered back to the shore. Sitting against a rock, I closed my eyes.

I was doing it. I was actually trekking in the Himalayas, by myself. No one tried to stop me. The women with headscarves and baskets that I passed along the way smiled at me and nodded.

"Namaste," they said.

The few tourists I encountered who were trekking with guides greeted me politely. They also left me alone. They carried only a day pack or a water bottle while the porters carried their gear. I felt smug. I was stronger than they were. Maybe I could be the next Alexandra David-Néel, crossing the Himalayas on foot at nineteen. I imagined myself chatting with the Australian trekkers. "Oh yes," I'd say, "Everest Base Camp. A beautiful trek . . . I was there in '96." Maybe from here I'd go on to Thailand. Maybe I'd go back to India. The sun beat down on my face. The river roared. A breeze stirred my hair. I fell asleep.

I wasn't sure how long I dozed. I didn't have a watch. When I woke up, the sun was far to the West. Frantically, I pulled on my dirty socks and tied my dusty boots. I grabbed my pack and hurried up the trail as my good mood disintegrated into worry. How much farther did I have to go?

The previous night, I had read that Buddhism was first introduced to Tibet in the seventh century. Tibetan kings invited Buddhist masters from India to help eradicate the old Bon religion, an indigenous blend of animism and nature worship. The arrival of Buddhism threatened the old ways. Younger generations saw Bon practices as backwards and shameful. Tensions broke out between traditional priests and Buddhist monks. These tensions became the basis for the stories of demon taming and mythical beings like Padmasambhava.

Coming from a Nazarene background, Buddhist stories of mountain gods reminded me of the Old Testament, of Jehovah and the rebellious Israelites who worshiped pagan gods. I never identified with a nomadic culture wandering through the desert. Growing up, deserts seemed far away and unreal. The thought of living in tents and eating mana from heaven never stirred my curiosity. But the colorful wall hangings of flying mystics and tall mountains did.

Climbing the ridge from the Khimti River, my mind fell to stories of the demon sisters who settled in this region. *Which mountains did they settle in?* I wondered. Scanning the skyline, I could just make out a few white peaks. I wished I knew their names.

Relentless, the trail continued up and up. I had been hiking for hours. *How much longer to the top?* I had to be on Deurali Pass. *How far have I climbed? What is my elevation?* I stared at my boots, willing them up the trail. Step—breathe—step—breathe.

Gradually, clouds moved in. A cold wind picked up. My mood, confident and happy a few hours ago, now plunged into misery. Did I think I liked trekking? No, I hated trekking. The mountains looked suddenly dark and oppressive. I imagined evil spirits hiding among the trees. I could almost see their grinning faces and slanted eyebrows. I was cold, thirsty, and ravenously hungry. Another hour passed and still, I climbed up and up. I hadn't seen anyone on the trail. Was I going the right way? Was I headed to Bhandar?

Pausing to wipe the sweat from my forehead, I glanced back. My lunch spot on the river had disappeared into the vast valley. All I could see was the dark fold of green where I had slept. Beyond that lay waves upon waves of forested foothills and white peaks. I took a gulp from my water bottle. Dark clouds hung low above my head. A spatter of rain hit my cheek. Hastily, I shoved my bottle into the nylon mesh pocket. It was getting late. Why had I slept along the riverbank? A sob caught in my throat. *Calm down, Julie. Breathe, breathe, breathe.*

Suddenly, the ground leveled off. I blinked and looked around—Deurali Pass. I was standing on a smooth, windswept knob high above the tree line. In front of me sat a stone structure with a thatched roof. Giant yaks with shaggy blond fur ambled around the courtyard. A hand-painted sign read, "Cheese Factory."

Cheese sounded divine. My stomach rumbled. Collapsing on a bench, I looked around. I was alone except for the yaks. A sharp wind whistled around the hut, bringing with it a fine, silvery rain. Shivering, I reached into my pack for my wool sweater.

"Hello?" An old man stood before me. He bowed and handed me a glass of jiggling white lumps.

I accepted his gift gratefully. I took a sip—yak yogurt. The cool, sour cream coated my tongue—lovely. I gulped the curds, my spirits lifting as the protein hit my stomach. Bhandar was downhill from here. Just another hour to go. I would make it. I rose to my feet.

"Namaste." Grinning, I handed the old man a crumpled ten rupee note.

He tucked the note into the folds of his coat, pointed down the other side of the pass, and said, "Bhandar."

"Bhandar?" I repeated.

He nodded, encouraging.

"Bhandar," I whispered to myself. Almost there. At the edge of the pass, I stopped to adjust my pack. I looked down. Far below sat a settlement of houses. They looked lonely in the rain.

"Better get a move on?" A man called out from behind me.

I jumped. It was an American trekker who looked to be in his mid-thirties. He had a pale face and wore his black hair in a ponytail. He patted the rainfly that covered his pack. "You got one of these?"

I hadn't even thought of bringing a rainfly. I shook my head.

He smiled, clicking a pair of trekking poles together. "You alone?"

"Kind of." I cinched up my hip belt and walked on.

"What's *kind of alone?*"

"I'm meeting up with someone in Bhandar," I lied.

His gaze hardened as he swung into step behind me. "I'm on holiday."

"Uh-huh." I walked a little faster, my toes digging into the front of my boots. Blisters had already formed on the top of my toes. Every step burned.

"Where you from?"

"Washington State."

"What are you doing out here?" His trekking poles clicked with every step.

"Trekking."

"I can see that," he said.

"Holiday from what?" I steered the conversation away from me.

"I live in Laos. Thought I'd come to Nepal for a vacation." Click, click.

"That's nice."

"Yep, gotta get back before Christmas."

"Really? Why's that?"

"Got a nice Vietnamese girl back in Laos."

"Mmm," I said. I walked faster.

"So, why's a young girl like you out here by yourself?" He was persistent.

"Trekking," I said again. My heart thudded. Fear prickled my skin.

"Well, you shouldn't be." He cleared his throat loudly and spat into the bushes. "That's the problem with American women," he added with a note of contempt. "They're too damned independent."

"What about your girlfriend?" I glanced back at him.

"She's Vietnamese." He grinned. "Skinny and obedient, the way women used to be."

I turned away, feigning nonchalance. Something about him didn't feel right. I felt ugly and oversized. I wasn't skinny and obedient. I had acne and thick legs.

"Strong legs," my sister, Jennifer, always said, "even though they're thick."

Jennifer had thin legs. Thin was beautiful. Blond was beautiful. Thick was ugly. Short dirty-blond hair was ugly. I was around eight when I first realized that. My dad was in his biking phase, trying to lose weight. He biked thirty-five miles a day.

"You could use some biking, kiddo." He pinched my belly.

I was confused. "Am I fat?"

"No, sweetie. You're not fat. But you and I have to watch our weight. We're built the same."

The words stuck. I was fat. Was it bad to be fat? I didn't think of my dad as fat. I loved his belly. I used to press my cheek against it when I sat on his lap. It felt warm and comforting, just like his dark-brown beard and curly hair.

But fat was bad, and it was bad to look like a boy with dirty-blond hair. Suddenly, I was ashamed. How could I have not known? I *was* ugly. Maybe I could be good and kind. Jesus said to love your neighbors as yourself. He also said blessed are the peacekeepers because theirs was the kingdom of heaven. Maybe I could be a peacekeeper. I would make a good peacekeeper. If I was good, maybe it would make up for being ugly and fat.

As I trotted down the trail with the American on my heels, I was grateful for my ugly appearance. I wore an oversized wool sweater that made me look plain and huge. That was good. I was glad I had acne and dirty-blond hair. Maybe the man would leave me alone. When we staggered into the village, I breathed a sigh of relief.

"This looks alright," the American said, pausing at the first guesthouse we came to. "You coming?"

"I don't think so."

The man clicked his trekking poles. "Suit yourself."

I hurried on, half-running. My ears strained backward for the sound of his poles. All remained quiet.

The trail ran through a wide-open field dotted with Sherpa houses. Whitewashed walls glowed in the darkness. Warm yellow light spilled from the windows. Great brown Tibetan dogs growled as I passed.

I stopped at the last guesthouse on the edge of town and peeked through the window. A round Sherpa woman with a striped apron leaned over a cookstove. When I knocked at the door, she greeted me with exclamations of surprise. Was it the late hour or at my being alone? Speaking rapidly in Tibetan, she drew me in. She fussed over my pack and muddy boots.

"Ah . . . you girl." She shook her head. "Come."

I followed her up the dark stairs to a small room next to the family's living quarters. As I passed an open door, I glimpsed two small boys playing with a gray kitten. Sacks of grain and shelves of dishes lined the room. Family. Children. Safety.

"You stay. Here." The woman motioned me into the room.

I let my pack fall to the floor. A low bed lay just under the windowsill. Through the window, I could see the white outline of Buddhist stupa shining in the moonlight. I smiled. I would sleep looking at the stars.

"You hurry, yes?" The woman pointed downstairs. She must want me to join them for dinner.

I sat at the table, where she handed me a bowl of steaming noodles with green nettles. I sipped the salty broth. It felt warm in the kitchen. The fire crackled in the round clay oven. The woman stirred the coals and said something to one of the children. Others soon arrived, shuffling their feet and stealing glances at me. She handed them bowls of soup. They sat on the floor, next to the fire and ate loudly. The woman made *tsking* sounds, but she smiled as she bustled around. The children laughed and talked rapidly. I couldn't understand them, but it was comforting to be with a family. I listened to the domestic sounds, clicking bowls, occasional laughter, the shaggy brown dog who wandered in and settled near the fire. I sighed. I wanted to stay here forever.

Later, I curled up in my sleeping bag and wrote notes in my journal by candlelight. Outside, a clear night sky stretched dark and silent over the hills. The moon hung low on the horizon. In the distance, I could hear the sounds of families getting ready for bed. Children cried and were hushed. Dogs barked. Men coughed and spat. Although I couldn't see Everest from here, I could feel the presence of the mountain. There was a sense of something in the cold, crisp air. Something unseen. Whatever it was, it was imminent, as though the mountain were drawing me into its arms. I thought about the creepy American. I hoped I wouldn't see him tomorrow. Maybe I should leave early. Maybe I should leave late. I fell asleep dreaming of empty passes and the wind whispering in my ears.

CHAPTER SIX

◁⫘●⫘◉⫘◉◉◉⫘●⫘▷

SUNLIGHT HIT MY FACE. I rolled over and peeked out the window. *Where am I?* Squinting, I recognized the stupa with its slanted Buddha eyes. Bhandar. I was in the Sherpa village of Bhandar on my way to Ringmo to find the Jirels. I'd overslept. Swinging my bare feet to the cold floor, I fumbled for my clothes. I pulled on my red dress and smoothed my wild hair. Cramming my sleeping bag and journal into my pack, I hurried downstairs.

Outside in the courtyard, the Sherpa woman was clearing plates from the table. When she saw me, she clicked her tongue and nodded toward the trail. The other trekkers must have left hours ago. I smiled.

She thrust a menu in my face. "Eat."

"Omelet?" I pointed to the words *ginger omelet*. I'd never had one of those. Homestays like this had the strangest combinations of Western food—dishes like ginger and masala omelets or oat porridge with apple. Over time, most households along the main trekking route became tourist stays. A family could easily turn an old storeroom into a guest bedroom or rent out a whole floor. Women ran the households while their husbands worked away as guides or porters. The extra income gave women more power. They were able to send their kids to school and fix up their homes.

I sat at the table and looked around. The guesthouse was perched on the far edge of a sloping meadow. Behind me stood the dark ridge that I had hiked down the previous night. Before me lay fields of barley and rye. They seemed to disappear over the edge of a vast expanse. Spreading out my map, I traced the trail I planned to take. It looked like I would cross the river before the next village. I should be able to reach Sete by midafternoon.

"Omelet." The Sherpa woman sat a plate in front of me with a thump.

I smiled and put my hands together. "*Namaste.* Coffee?"

She clicked her tongue and disappeared into the kitchen. Returning moments later with a large carafe, she sat across from me and leaned forward.

"You trek alone?"

"Yes." I took a bite of the omelet.

She made that *tsking* sound again and shook her head.

"You live alone?" I asked.

"Yes. Ah, my husband, he dies in avalanche on mountain." She pointed at the trail. "Everest."

"I'm so sorry."

"I work hard . . . but," she said, smiling, "is much better."

"Much better?" Did she mean that being single was better than being married or that she was doing better now? A child wailed from somewhere inside her house.

"You go." The Sherpa woman stood, motioning for me to hurry.

I gulped down the rest of my coffee and omelet and reached for my pack.

"You. Come. Again." She said the words distinctly while gripping my hand in hers. Her skin felt warm and leathery.

"I will," I said. "On my way back in . . ." *When will I be back? A few days? A week? Two weeks?* "Soon."

"Okay. You go Sete." She shooed me away.

I waved goodbye and started down the trail. She probably thought I was crazy for getting such a late start. I wasn't worried. I could hike fast.

My stiff legs warmed under the weight of my pack. I was getting used to it; the pack felt like an old friend. It was my first gear purchase, something I had bought at an REI in Portland with my dad. It was a Mountain Hardware design, black with teal pouches and a yellow nylon mesh.

"She's going to the Himalayas," my dad had told the young, ruddy-cheeked salesclerk. "She needs something good."

"Please, Dad," I whispered.

"What?" he asked loudly. "You do."

The salesclerk smiled. "Are you a mountaineer?"

"She's an anthropologist," Dad replied for me. "Someone who studies people. She's going to do research."

I think I bought the pack just so he'd quit talking. At least he wasn't telling everyone I was a missionary. Secretly, I was pleased. My dad was proud of me. Maybe someday it would be okay with my father that I wasn't a Christian.

Dad was the worship leader at our church. Every Sunday, he left early on his Yamaha to practice with the band. On weekends when I was home from college, I went with him even though I didn't want to. Sometimes we talked about my faith—or lack of it.

"You do believe in God," Dad would say. "I know you do."

"Maybe," I'd hedge.

"But, Julie," my mom would say, "it's the way you were raised. Why don't you believe?"

I tried to explain about anthropology, how we learned to see other cultures through the people's eyes, not our own. "It's called cultural relativism, Mom. We try to understand people from their own culture. How can we expect them to believe like us?"

My mother shook her head thoughtfully. "I don't know, Julie."

It was never an overt conflict but something that mystified my parents. They grew up in their church. They'd always believed. Their parents had believed. Their grandparents had believed. Everyone in my family believed. Everyone but me.

I made it to the river within a few hours—a great splashing river with silvery sand and chaotic boulders. I dropped my pack. I flipped off my boots. I ate some trail mix and a Power Bar. I sat in the sun and closed my eyes. This was everything I'd dreamed of. No missionaries, no church. Nobody to tell me what to do or where to go. It was pure freedom. And to my relief, I didn't run into that creepy American. In fact, I hadn't seen anyone on the trail. Was that a good thing or bad?

The trail across the river was a thin, well-defined track that ran back and forth up the mountainside. Something was missing: a bridge. I stood and looked around. The trail on this side of the river was overgrown with bushes and tall grass. *This isn't right. Where are the footprints?* I scanned the ground.

Grass that was taller than me blocked my vision. I could see the distant mountain peaks but nothing near me. Sweating, I wiped my face with the back of my hand. There were two trails, one on my side of the river and one on the other side. But I didn't see a bridge. Which trail was I supposed to take? I retraced my steps up the winding path. Now, I could see a bridge—a few gray planks of wood strung together with rope and suspended by a rusty cable. It didn't look safe. But it was a bridge.

I grabbed my pack. Branches slapped my face as I fought through the underbrush. *Do people actually use this bridge?* Glancing back at the small sandy beach, my mind raced. *Am I supposed to cross here?* The planks were spaced about a foot apart. I could easily fall through them if I wasn't careful. I took a deep breath and stepped onto the first plank. The contraption vibrated. I gripped the rope rails with my sweaty palms. *What if the cable snaps?* I took a few steps. The bridge sagged and swayed under my weight. I glanced down. The river rushed between my boots. An icy breeze blew against my legs. *Don't look down. Don't look down. Should I go back?*

I glanced over my shoulder. I was halfway across. *Keep going. Keep going.* I clutched the rails and inched over the rotting planks, pausing when the bridge swung too far. Stumbling onto the solid ground, I sobbed with relief.

Looking back, I shook my head. I would never cross that bridge again. There had to be another way. A steep climb would be better than that thing. I walked. Each step carried me farther up the mountain. The hot sun beat down on my skin. Sweat dripped down my back. My feet felt like lead. Step, step, step. My mind grew numb with the effort. I quit thinking about anything except getting up the mountain. There was nothing in this world but up.

I climbed for hours. At last, I stopped to catch my breath. I looked around. Below me, the canyon fell straight down. The forested hills folded up tightly against the gorge I had just crossed. I understood now why trekking in the Himalayas was different than anywhere else. There was no such thing as flat ground. In the North Cascades, you could hike along the crest. The ridge ran north to south. Here, the mountains ran east to west. The big rivers cut through them. To get anywhere, you had to descend to the river, then climb up thousands of feet. It was maddening.

I arrived at a slight plateau. A few houses with gardens lay scattered across the hillside. Maybe I could find a teahouse. *Where are the other trekkers? I should have run into someone by now. What time is it?* I glanced up at the sun. *Maybe three or four in the afternoon. Why am I not in Sete?*

I stopped to rest under the shade of a spindly tree. I dug inside for my map and water bottle. I spread the map on my lap and looked for Sete. The red trail disappeared within the folds. My map had torn. I couldn't make out where I'd crossed the river. I traced the route from Bhandar to Sete. I should be there by now. *Where am I?*

A rooster crowed. I was sitting in the entrance to someone's vegetable garden. I peeked through a hedge of beans. Chickens scratched in the dirt. A goat lay tethered to a post. I waited. Another trekker had to be coming soon. A wind whipped my hair. It was hot. I was almost out of water. Minutes passed. Flies landed on my arms. I flicked them off. I looked down the trail. I looked up the trail. No one.

I stood. *Where is everyone?* Closing my eyes, I strained to hear the sound of rushing water. Nothing. *Where am I? Was that someone's footsteps?* I turned at the sound. An old man with a basket of wood upon his head limped toward me.

"Please," I said. "How long to Sete?" I held out my map. "Sete."

The old man frowned and shook his head. "No, Sete, *didi*. Pike!" He pronounced it like the ballet term—*piqué*.

"Pike?" I whispered, my heart sinking.

"Yes, Pike." He pointed up the trail. "Pike, Pike."

I took in a deep breath then let it out slowly. I couldn't believe it. "No, sir, please. Sete. I must go to Sete."

The old man coughed before spitting into a bush. Glaring at me through deep-set eyes, he frowned. The dirty creases on his face looked shiny in the hot sun. I jumped as he yelled out the word again: "Pike!"

I shook my head. Ignoring me, the old man continued up the trail. I gazed down at my map. Tears stung my eyes. I searched for any place that started with a *P*, but I saw nothing. My hands shook. *What do I do now?*

"Sir! Please, sir!"

The old man had his back to me. "Pike . . . Pike . . . Pike . . .," he muttered as he plodded away.

Placing my hand over my chest, I said a small prayer. I had chosen the wrong trail back at the river. I had no idea where I was. If I turned back now, I'd never make it to Sete before dark. I didn't want to cross that bridge at night. My headlamp was a dim little thing. My batteries were weak. There was no way I could find my way in the dark. A wave of panic washed over me as my predicament became clear.

I was alone.

I was nineteen.

I was lost in the Himalayas.

CHAPTER SEVEN

◁❏●❏❏◉❏◉◉◉◉❏◉❏●❏❏▷

WHEN I WAS THIRTEEN, my sister ran away from home.

"Did she leave a note?" Dad turned away, but I saw his tears. She was just gone. "No." I bit my lip.

Dad called the police. "We have a runaway. My daughter's missing."

Runaway made her sound like someone else. Was my sister a runaway? What did that even mean?

Mom dropped her purse. She couldn't find her keys. Dad kept shaking his head. "Where'd you put the car keys, Ann!"

The taillights bounced on the driveway. I didn't want to be alone when the police arrived. The house felt big and empty.

A couple of miles from our farm, a dirt road ran into the hills. There was a creek, an old homestead, and an aspen grove where I had seen bears, coyotes, porcupines, and deer. I walked there almost every day. That was where I wanted to go now.

I grabbed my sweater and ran outside. Fading sunlight lit the hills. It was early May. Meadowlarks sang. I could smell sagebrush and pine trees. Green hills rose into the fading blue sky on either side of me. Nighthawks swooped down for insects. Crickets hummed in the grass. As I crested a hill, the dirt road leveled into a broad valley surrounded by steep ridges and forest. An abandoned, white-washed homesteader's cabin sat nestled in the field. An overgrown lilac bush grew in the yard. Blue curtains fluttered in the open windows. I was just about to peek in the windows when a strange, snarling scream pierced the air. It was a cougar.

I froze, my eyes scanning the hills. Nothing. Silence. Again, a high-pitched scream. *Where is he? By the house? Under the house?* My heart pounded. My legs trembled. I couldn't move. *Can he see me?* I couldn't see him.

I was alone. My parents didn't know where I was. Nobody did. When would they notice I had left? They were looking for Jennifer, not me. They were always looking for Jennifer. A small part of me hoped that the cougar would attack. I imagined my parents finding me mutilated, half-eaten. Maybe dead. *Would they cry? How many people would call on the telephone? Would the church ladies bring potluck meals? Would they finally notice me?*

Standing on a mountainside in the Himalayas, watching the little man trudge down the trail, I felt the same way as that day with the cougar. Dying in the Himalayas would be a romantic way to go. If I never came back, would my parents finally notice that I was gone for good?

But no. I was scared, and I wanted to go home. Fighting to hold myself together, I took a deep breath. *Don't panic. Breathe. Breathe. Think.*

When I ran into the cougar that night long ago, I did the only thing I knew. I choked down my fears, backed up slowly, then ran like hell. My parents never knew I had left the house.

A rooster crowed, breaking my reverie. *Pike.* The man had said Pike. *What is Pike? Is it a settlement or a village? Maybe I could make it there before dark.*

I climbed for another half an hour or so. Waves of fear rolled over me. *What if I can't find Pike?* The trail didn't look like a trail that led to a town. It looked more like a cat-track.

Clouds moved in. The wind picked up. I could smell the coming rain. The trail entered a forest. Tall rhododendrons, with twisting trunks, loomed in the gray twilight. Vines curled around oak and pine trees. Tangled roots and rotting leaves covered the path. I imagined Tibetan gods with their grinning faces and pointed ears. I tripped. Falling to my knees, I started to cry. No tears and my mouth felt like cotton. It was almost dark. *Why did I come all this way on my own? What am I trying to prove?*

A sound. *What was that?* I held my breath. *People?* I leaped to my feet. The voices grew louder as I walked. Trekkers. They were just a few feet ahead, sitting alongside the trail. Six of them. A jolly-looking man with gray hair and a beard. A woman with short hair, who passed around crackers and cheese. Trekking poles and fanny packs rested against a tree. An entourage of porters stood off to one side, loaded with supplies and camping gear.

I called out. "Hello?"

"*Bonjour,*" they said at the same time.

"Where are you headed?" I asked.

"*Nous allons, Pike,*" the woman with short gray hair said. "*Et vous?*"

"I'm so sorry," I said. "I'm lost and—"

"*Parlez-vous Français?*"

"No," I replied.

"Ah, our English is . . ." The woman with short hair shrugged. "Very little."

One of the men frowned. "You are *seul,* alone?"

"Yes," I replied.

"Ah . . . you come us."

"Yes, please." I laughed. What a relief. I was saved.

The group leader was a tall, handsome woman who spoke Nepali as well as French. She glared at me before turning to one of the porters. After a heated discussion, she jerked her head toward me.

"*Cependant, nous montons Pike; vous devres aller a Junbesi sur votre proper.*" *We are climbing Pike. You will have to go to Junbesi on your own.*

So, Pike was a mountain, not a town.

"*Vous pouvez venir avec nous ce soir.*" *You may go with us tonight.*

I nodded. I understood the stupidity of my actions, and now I was at their mercy. I felt lightheaded and strange. The trees shimmered oddly around me. My head ached. I felt hot and cold at the same time. My heart raced irregularly.

We continued up the trail. I stumbled and tried to keep up. I stumbled again. The jolly man was having a hard time too. He kept stopping to breathe. The short-haired woman patted his shoulder and waited with him.

Darkness fell. The porters lit lamps and called for us to hurry. We struggled up, up, and up. Finally, we made it to the pass. Someone nudged me toward a small brick building. The rain was coming. I could smell it. I had reached Goli Gompa.

I sat before the fire in an old monastery kitchen. Two nuns, wearing maroon-colored robes, fed the fire and stirred the soup. Brown skin and laugh lines surrounded their eyes. One handed me a bowl of soup and smiled.

"*Dhan'yavada.*" *Thank you,* I said.

Outside, the French laughed and talked loudly. The porters had set up their tents in the courtyard. Now, they sat around a campfire drinking wine and waiting for their meal. They were having grilled steaks and potatoes. One of the porters had brought a cheesecake.

I was sick of noodle soup. Steak and potatoes would have been wonderful. Instead, I sipped my broth. My cheeks felt hot and swollen. *A sunburn. Do I have a fever?*

The nuns hurried into the night. I glanced around the room. Stone walls gave the monastery a castlelike feel. Small windows with green shutters faced the night sky. A red rug covered the floor. A four-year old calendar hung on a wall. A Tibetan god stared back at me. I looked down at my soup. I wanted to be outside with everyone else. I set my bowl on the floor and grabbed my sweater.

Stars glittered overhead. The monastery was perched on top of a rounded knoll. Moonlight illuminated the surrounding hills and peaks. The valleys lay deep in shadows. A stone wall ran around the courtyard. I sat with my knees tucked under my chin. Down the trail, the porters whistled while they set up tents. Someone played a harmonica. I could smell rice cooking.

By the sound of it, the French had finished several bottles of wine. Their hearty laughter spilled into the night. I felt lonely. Everyone had a group but me. I glanced at the porter's fire. They huddled near it, talking quietly. I watched as they blew on their hands and stomped their feet. *Maybe I could join them.*

Taking a deep breath, I walked toward the fire. A man with curly hair smiled at me. He put his arm around my shoulder and welcomed me into the circle. Everyone shifted to make room. They smiled at each other. I looked down. *What do they think of me? A young American girl lost in the mountains.* I expected them to shake their heads or *tsk* like the Sherpa woman. Instead, the porters just laughed and patted me on the back. They spoke rapidly in Sherpa. They gestured at my back. *Are they asking about my heavy pack?* We stood around the fire, nodding and smiling. I couldn't understand a word they said, but it was nice to hear their voices. When their food was ready, they invited me to stay.

"You eat?" the curly-haired porter asked.

I shook my head. "I go to bed."

He leaned over and kissed my cheek. I started and stepped away. The other porters laughed and made whistling sounds. The curly-haired porter was not much older than me. He grinned and gave me a hug. I turned away. Maybe the darkness would hide my smile. Would I see him tomorrow?

I lay awake inside my sleeping bag. The nuns were asleep on their cots. Soft snores filled the room. A shaft of moonlight from an open window fell on a picture of Miyolangsangma, the goddess of Mount Everest. She sat on her golden tiger and watched me from her snowy peak. Beneath her lay trees and river valleys. I thought about the dark forest I had climbed through today.

I awoke to the sound of chanting. A *lama* wearing a dark robe and a jacket buttoned up to his throat paced the room. As he walked back and forth, he swung a pot of incense through the air and gray smoke curled around him. The scent of juniper filled the room. After several minutes of chanting, the lama sat near the kitchen fire. One of the nuns handed him a cup. I lay still for a few minutes, relishing the warmth of my sleeping bag. I wanted the man to go away so I could dress.

Today, I would leave for Junbesi. The Frenchwoman had found me a guide. I had no idea how far the town was, or where I would stay the night. It was hard to communicate. Nepali, Tibetan, Sherpa, French—it all blew right by me.

The lama rose and ambled outside. The aroma of cooking oil filled the room. I pulled my dress over my head and wiggled out of my long underwear. I walked over to the fire. The nun handed me a cup of hot tea. I watched her shape round dough into flat disks. Her hands flew as she tossed the dough between her fingers, slap, slap, slap. I was just about to ask her where I could find my guide when a young man wearing a blue North Face fleece ducked through the doorway. He had short hair and a wide, pleasant smile.

"Gandji." He bowed.

He must be my guide. He turned to the nun and spoke rapidly in Nepali. The nun laughed and shook her head. They both looked at me. *What are they saying?* I tried to look strong and confident. The nun handed me a hot fried cake and motioned for me to go. I grabbed my stuff and followed Gandji out the door.

Outside, I caught my breath. We were standing on a high ridgeline, surrounded by dozens of white peaks. Perched on the tip of the ridge sat a monastery with smoke drifting into the blue sky. Colorful prayer flags fluttered in the breeze. Deep ravines fell away into green river valleys. I was on top of the world.

A layer of frost covered the tents in the courtyard. The French were just waking up. The woman with short hair gave me a cheerful wave. *"Bonjour."*

"Morning." I pointed at the mountains.

"Beautiful," she said. "Today we climb Pike."

"Yes," I said. "Good luck."

Gandji pointed to the trail. "We go." He tapped his walking stick on the ground.

I glanced around. The porter who'd kissed me last night was nowhere to seen. Sighing, I swung into step behind Gandji, leaving the Goli Gompa and the French behind.

We headed up the ridge toward the monastery. *Why another monastery? Why not Junbesi?* The stone building didn't look far. As I panted behind Gandji, my legs felt rubbery. I struggled to breathe in the thin air. Ever since yesterday, I felt strange— weak and sluggish. I doubled over. A sharp pain hit my gut.

Glancing over his shoulder, Gandji stopped walking. He motioned for my pack.

I shook my head. "I'm fine."

"I take," he said.

He grabbed my pack from me and draped it over his shoulder. My cheeks flamed. I always carried my own pack.

After what seemed like forever, we arrived at the monastery courtyard. Older women wearing bright handkerchiefs on their heads sat knitting in the sun. They clicked their tongues as their fingers flashed back and forth. When they saw us, they stopped and stared. They seemed to know Gandji. As for me, I was something of a curiosity.

An old man greeted Gandji with a hearty *"Namaste."* As they talked, the old man glanced over at me. Gandji pointed at the monastery. *Do they want me to go inside?*

I ducked into a dark room. The man led me up a narrow wooden staircase to a large square room. It took a moment for my eyes to adjust. A sliver of sunlight streamed through a small window. I saw a row of Buddha statues behind a low altar— legs crossed, hands folded under their chins or resting on their knees. A few stood taller than me. Others could have fit in my lap. I peered into their faces. When I looked into their eyes, they seemed real. One scowled. Another radiated serenity.

A large bell on the altar represented female energy. Next to it lay a *dorje*, a phallic-shaped metal object that symbolizes male energy and good luck. Twelve bowls of water were arranged in a neat line for the Buddhas to drink. At night, the lama emptied them. In the morning, he filled them. Dried fruit lay scattered across the altar for the Buddhas to eat.

Gandji removed his cap and murmured a prayer. *What do I do?* I bowed my head like I was in church. I wanted to kneel on the cold, dusty floor and gaze into the Buddhas' faces. They seemed to have something to say. I was embarrassed. *What right do I have to worship here?*

Growing up in the Nazarene church, I was taught that idolatry was evil. Catholics worshiped statues. And that was why, according to my grandmother, Catholics didn't go to heaven. In Sunday school, our teacher told us the story of Moses, who climbed Mount Sinai to receive the Ten Commandments. While he was gone, the Israelites danced and sang and fashioned a golden calf to worship.

"The Israelites disobeyed God, didn't they?" Our Sunday school teacher had said. "Does God exist in an image of stone?"

We shook our heads.

"Does God exist in images of gold?"

"No," we said.

"Because God is the unseen god, isn't he?"

"Yes," we said.

"God is the *Great I Am*."

"Yes." We shook our heads. Those rebellious Israelites would never learn.

Now, standing in the dark temple in the Himalayas, I sank to my knees. I looked at the Buddhas' faces. I liked the one in the middle. His heavy eyes were cast down. His lips curved in a benevolent smile. There was something familiar about his face. I had known it my whole life. Some of the statues frightened me, but this one was different. Tears pricked my eyelids. I wanted to kiss his feet, but I didn't.

There were many beautiful things about the Christianity of my childhood—the songs, feelings of forgiveness. But there was little room for physical beauty in the churches of my youth. Mostly, I remembered the plain, sad buildings with cheap linoleum kitchens and metal folding chairs. Even the altar was ugly, with microphones and wires and big outdated speakers. I wished I had grown up Catholic. They had cathedrals and paintings. They had robes and holy water. But Protestants rejected outward trappings of beauty and sacred images because they led to idolatry. Idolatry was a sin.

It was the lack of mystery in my church that I ran from. Everything was either black or white. I was either saved or not saved. I either believed or I didn't believe. Nothing ever sparked my imagination.

Now, staring into the Buddha's face, I felt something. I wasn't sure what. I knew it was just a plaster cast. If I pushed it over, it would break. The Buddha wasn't here anymore than Christ was. But something about this face intrigued me. I wanted peace. I wanted serenity. I wanted mystery—a mystery big enough to spend my life running after it.

That morning in the Himalayas, I was too young to understand that sacred images were a reference for something greater. I didn't understand that we often mistake the reference for the actual thing. The magical Buddha with his enigmatic smile had caught my imagination. It was something I could relate to. Something I could feel. Something tangible and sacred.

CHAPTER EIGHT

◁I□●I□I◙I◉I◉I◉I□I●□I▷

I GREW UP IN apple country, along the Columbia River in Washington State. We lived six miles from Bridgeport, where my father worked as a high-voltage electrician at the Chief Joseph Dam. A hundred years ago, white homesteaders had carved the orchards from dry, stony hills. During the '80s, migrant workers from faraway states in Mexico filled the stores with young men who smiled shyly and spoke to each other in soft, rapid Spanish. On Sunday mornings, I listened to them singing in the orchards around our church. I envied them. I wanted to be outside.

Aside from religion, my parents believed in the "great outdoors." By the time I was seven or eight, we had camped next to, or backpacked into, most of Washington's mountain lakes. Always organized, Mom kept our packs stocked with food, clothing, and our favorite reading book. Every Friday evening when Dad got home from work, we piled into the blue Dodge pickup and drove to the nearest trailhead.

My favorite place was Wolf Creek. We would hike in a couple of miles and set up camp next to the creek. Mom cooked dinner over the camp stove while Dad fished. After a meal of instant rice and trout, my sister and I would curl up in our sleeping bags. Jennifer usually read by flashlight, but I lay still, listening to the sounds outside. So much noise in the dark. Barred owls hoo-hooing, frogs croaking, and crickets chirping. Once, I heard a loud crash. Then, snuffling. I lay in suspense. *Is it a deer? A moose? A bear?*

Next to our camp stood a house-sized boulder that jutted into the water. In the afternoons, I lay on that rock and basked in the sun. When the cottonwoods released their seeds, bits of cotton floated through the air like snow. I felt safe, surrounded by willows and the deafening roar of the creek.

Backpacking, I learned the great solace of the earth. I learned the feeling of walking and an empty mind. I learned that walking, even when you don't feel like it, can calm your mind. After a day outside, my mind became cleaner, happier.

In the mornings, I loved waking up to the scent of brewing coffee and the sharp, sweet aroma of wet earth. In the afternoons, when the sun heated up the forest, I'd press my nose against the bark of a ponderosa pine. It smelled like baked vanilla, so warm and sweet I once put a bit of it in my mouth. It had a chemical taste, like something my mother used to polish floors. I loved the sunlight filtering through the trees. Shadows danced on the ground. There were roots and vines and craggy nooks to explore. Everywhere I turned, something moved—a rush of wings, the wind picking up or dying down. The sound of it in the treetops.

Barefoot, with my jeans rolled up, I wandered through the creeks. The polished rocks were slippery. I searched for minnows and crawdads. Sometimes I'd find little periwinkle cocoons, a mosaic of miniscule, mismatched rocks, no bigger than my pinkie. I'd stand in the creek until I couldn't feel my toes. Then, I would sit on the shore, flicking flies off my arms and drawing shapes in the sand. I was bored, but happy. The world seemed a pleasant place, timeless and still.

Wolf Creek gushed from the snow fields of Mount Gardner, nine miles and a lifetime away from my childhood afternoons.

I would not hike to the peak until years later, as a teenager, rediscovering the mountains on my own. Then, in-between shifts waiting tables, I would steal away and run up those old trails. I kept trying to find my way back to those afternoons. They lingered in the corners of my memory like a dream I couldn't shake. But I couldn't go back, and now everything was different.

Our life as a family fell apart when my sister turned from a headstrong, happy child into an angry, bitter teenager. She hated everyone, especially my parents. Her boyfriend smoked and didn't own a car. They fought over the boyfriend and over where she spent her time. They fought about the music she listened to and the clothes she wore. Jennifer and Dad clashed over everything. Their arguments erupted at every meal. At night, I fell asleep to their arguing. In the morning, I woke up to it.

My mother grew distant and sad. Her grief became palpable, like another being in the house. Sometimes, on our way to school in the morning, she wept as we walked away. I'd turn back to see her in her bathrobe, barefoot—like a little girl.

I tried to console her. "Are you okay, Mom?" I knew she wasn't. "It's okay, Mom. I love you." But it wasn't okay. And I couldn't make it so.

My sister told her friends that my dad was abusive. She said he lost his temper. I sat three seats ahead of her on the bus. *Stop talking, stop talking, stop talking,* I wanted to shout. But I said nothing. Instead, I pinched the fat on my stomach and measured the number of days it would take to make it disappear.

My sister's anger knew no bounds. She agreed to drive me to school if I paid for gas, but every morning she left early to hang out at her boyfriend's house. I would sit in the truck with the broken windows and watch the sun rise. My breath froze in the air. It seemed like forever. If I complained, she told me I could walk.

"Get out," she hissed once when I said something disparaging about her boyfriend. "Get out of my truck!"

"No!" I held my breath.

She slammed on the brakes, reached across me, and flung the door open. I stumbled out, tears of rage stinging my eyes.

"Screw you, Jen," I said. She was already gone, tires squealing and gravel hitting my face.

Sometimes I entered her room and looked at her things—paintings, her figurines, her favorite horse posters. I imagined ripping those posters to shreds. In my mind, I broke every one of her figurines, especially the ones we had picked out together when we were small. Or the ones I gave her for Christmas or her birthdays. I imagined the sound of breaking glass. I imagined putting my fist through her mirror. *What would it feel like? What sound would it make?* I closed my eyes and thought so hard, I almost believed I had done it. Then, I would open my eyes and see nothing—just the room and the sound of sprinklers chugging round and round in the alfalfa field.

It occurred to me then. *I could quit eating.* If I quit eating, maybe *they* would quit fighting. Maybe life would go back to normal. Maybe I would go back to normal. I couldn't name what was wrong with me. A certain hopelessness. A feeling of drifting. Sometimes when I lay on my back and looked at the sky, I imagined what it would be like to disappear. *What would it be like to be nothing?*

In junior high, sex was the paramount topic on everyone's mind. Everyone's but mine. That winter, the boys in our class climbed through the window of the girls' locker room. We were rated on a scale of one to ten. A boy named Donovan started it first. Deceptively sweet, with soft brown hair and wide dark eyes, he hoisted himself through the window. The others followed. They stood and gawked as we pretended to grab our clothes. We didn't really hurry. We took our time in various stages of undress, letting them see us. Where did we fall on their scale of beauty? It felt strange to let someone see you naked. Half of me was horrified. But a tiny part of me wanted to be seen. *Am I beautiful?*

Later, the results were passed around on a piece of paper. I sat at my desk, pretending not to notice. *How did I rate?* I wasn't thin or fat. I was average. One day, the secret paper landed on my desk. I saw my name. Almost last. Out of eleven girls, I was only prettier than one.

Some of us began dieting then, at only twelve or thirteen. We competed to see who could lose the most weight. No more lunches. I tossed my peanut butter and jelly sandwiches in the garbage. I nibbled on a carrot. Not all of the girls refused to eat. They gorged themselves on macaroni and cheese, green beans, and little boxes of milk. We, the dieters, felt superior and strong. *We* could exist without food.

At first it was fun. Just a game. But as the weeks and months wore on, it became something else. My waist shrunk, and so did my hips. Cleanliness became an obsession. I took showers every morning and evening. Toilets disgusted me, especially at school. I would hold it until I returned home. Even at home, I bleached the seat before I sat down.

One morning, Donovan, the boy with brown eyes, caught me alone in the hallway. He shoved me into the lockers. "How do you like it?"

I was afraid of Donovan. He talked about skinning squirrels and chipmunks for fun. He described how drowning kittens would struggle. He laughed about it. He would laugh and laugh until his eyes teared. I didn't always believe him. I couldn't imagine that he would actually kill all the animals he talked about. *Is he joking or not?*

Today, his eyes glinted. "How about it?"

"Get off!" I shoved him as hard as I could.

"No, really. How do you like it?" His fingers dug into my skin as he tried to get his hands down my pants.

"You're disgusting." I hissed. "Get off me."

"Everyone else wants it." He leaned in closer. "What's wrong with you, Julie?"

What is *wrong with me?* The days drifted by in perpetual twilight. Everything revolved around calories. I rationed out the calories, adding them meticulously in a notebook beside my bed. I memorized the caloric intake of all the food in our house. Apples, sixty calories. Toast without butter, a hundred calories. A peanut butter sandwich, four hundred calories. Definitely out of the question. I tried to eat no more than four hundred calories each day. I allowed myself one bite of toast for breakfast and an apple for lunch. Dinner was problematic, as my parents plied me with food.

"Julie, have some more," Mom would say, passing me the beef stroganoff.

"Yeah, have some butter on your bread," Dad would add.

I pushed the food around on my plate, pretending to eat while I waited for the opportunity to slip everything into the garbage.

One night, I had a brilliant idea. Mom had bought Tupperware cups for everyday use. I filled a cup halfway with milk. After spitting my chewed food into the half-filled cup, I dumped it down the garbage disposal. It worked beautifully. I pretended to eat, and my parents were pleased that I drank so much milk.

I attended ballet classes. As I *pliéd*, *relevéd*, and *tendued*, I watched myself in the mirror, sucking in my stomach as hard as I could. I was a terrible dancer. By late afternoon, my head felt like it was stuffed with cotton. My legs felt rubbery.

I could hardly see straight, much less pirouette or leap across the studio. I persisted. The repetitive exercise and counting by fours and eights fed the same satisfaction as calculating calories and deprivation.

I had so many goals. Goals to lose five pounds. Then ten pounds. Twenty pounds. I had goals for the diameter of my waist and goals for my hips and thighs. My self-control was enormous. I could do anything by not eating. At school, I rose on the scale of beauty. I went from tenth place to second. Thin was beautiful.

Years later, I found my way back up Wolf Creek. It was a hot summer afternoon. I stood in the forest and listened. It was the same spot where I had played as a child. I heard the wind in the cottonwoods. I could almost hear my sister and me laughing in the creek. For a second, I had that feeling of everything being *alright*. That the world was beautiful and safe. No violence or sadness. I wanted to go back. I had survived junior high, but something inside me was broken. Something that would never be whole again.

CHAPTER NINE

⊲❑❒❍◉❍❑◉❍◉❍◉❍❑❍◉❑❍⊳

THAT MORNING IN THE Himalayas, I felt a sense of peace. Butter lamps burned on the altar. Shadows danced on the Buddhas' faces. It was quiet. Just the sound of my heart beating and the hiss of flames in the dark.

Buddhists believe that by following the eight-fold path—a guide for ethical living—you attain enlightenment. Right action, right speech, right concentration. It seemed like a practical way to gain inner peace. I'd never understood the Christian belief in being saved. It didn't seem fair that someone who lived a terrible life could ask for forgiveness at the last minute and go to heaven.

I made my way downstairs. Stepping outside, the bright sun nearly blinded me. Gandji grabbed my pack and motioned to the nearby lama. I handed the man a ten rupee note. Putting my hands together, I bowed.

"Dhan'yavada," I said.

Temples like this didn't get many visitors. Famous monasteries like Tengboche, on the way to Everest, received hundreds. They relied on tourist donations, but who would find this tiny temple, days off the beaten track? In Tibet, the eldest brother inherited the family's land. The younger brother usually became a monk. This tradition kept the land from being divided into smaller pieces as the family grew larger. It also fed a thriving monastic community. The boys were sent away at twelve or thirteen years old. Families supported their sons with gifts of food and money. In return, they gained honor from their son's achievements in monastic life. Monks learned to read and write. They memorized long prayers and verses. They studied subjects like debate and philosophy.

Gandji started down the mountainside. I followed. *What if the youngest son doesn't want to become a monk?* I was the youngest daughter. What if I had to become a nun? What if I couldn't choose what to do with my life? Then again, maybe having my future decided for me would be nice. Everyone told me I could do anything. I'd read enough Joseph Campbell to know that I wanted to follow my bliss. *But what is my bliss?* In a world of endless opportunities, how would I ever know that I'd chosen the right path?

The trail wound down a rocky ridgeline before entering a dark forest. Gandji walked quickly, swinging his arms. I kept my eyes on the trail as it zigzagged—now in the sun, now in the shade. We walked like this for hours—Gandji striding ahead and me hurrying behind. The trees shifted and sighed in the wind. Sometimes we stopped for water. There was nothing in the world but sun and trail, forest and shade.

All the while, my stomach cramped randomly. Spots swam before my eyes. My legs felt detached from my body. *Will we ever stop?* Abruptly, the trail emerged from the forest and climbed straight up into the sun. I closed my eyes against the harsh light. *Not another pass.* Gandji paused to look at me. He pointed to the highest point on the ridge. Shading my eyes, I could just make out the crumbling white bricks of a monastery. Prayer flags fluttered against the blue sky. Another climb.

I stared at my hiking boots, willing them up the trail. I had to make it to the top. I couldn't give up now. Step ... breathe ... step

. . . breathe. After a while, I saw Gandji's blue fleece disappear over the high ridge. A few more steps, and I was at the top.

The wind almost knocked me over. Prayer flags whipped above my head. Peering over the other side, a thin outline of a river gleamed far below.

"Junbesi." Gandji held up his finger. "One day more."

The view was even more spectacular than from Goli Gompa. Mountains disappeared into mountains. Peaks folded into valleys. Rivers ran between them. Gazing out at the horizon, I felt small and insignificant. The mountains were beautiful, but somehow they made me sad. *Who am I in all this beauty?* I felt lost in the sheer enormity of the landscape. I was nothing. Attached to nobody. It was both exhilarating and terrifying.

Across the courtyard, a lama dozed in the sunlight. When Gandji shouted, his face broke into a wide smile. Bowing and nodding, they greeted each other like old friends. Gandji followed the man inside. Glancing around, I found a spot out of the wind and sat. I pulled out my map, tracing the dotted red line from Goli Gompa. *This must be Ngor lamasery.* It was a tiny dot on the southern edge of Solu Khumbu.

A shadow fell across my lap. A plump, older woman smiled down at me. She held out a glass of something. I smiled and took a sip. *Apple juice? Or wine?* I couldn't tell, but it tasted bubbly and sweet. The plump woman made that *tsking* sound as she hovered over me, watching me drink. When I finished, she patted my head. I sighed and leaned back against the stone wall. I felt sleepy. Across the courtyard, Gandji and the old man wandered out. Their voices rose and fell on the wind as they sat, drinking out of large mugs. The sun beat down on my face. The wind whistled above my head. It was warm. I slept.

I awoke to Gandji's face peering into mine. He looked concerned. "We stay." He pointed to the building. *Did I oversleep? Are we supposed to keep hiking?*

I followed Gandji into a bright shrine room. A large Buddha statue sat behind an altar. Incense and butter lamps burned at its feet. Gandji pointed to a wide bench under a row of windows. "Here." He motioned at my sleeping bag. As I arranged my bag, the plump woman shuffled in and began emptying the water bowls. She muttered a chant as she worked, dusting the area around the bowls and lighting a stick of incense.

Unlike the strict monastic traditions of the larger monasteries, lamas presided over these rural temples. These religious practitioners performed rituals and ceremonies for everyday occasions. The lamas could marry and have children. The plump woman was the lama's wife, and the small child peeking around the doorframe was their granddaughter.

When the woman left, Gandji came over and knelt beside me. Taking my hands, he twisted them into a meditating pose and sprinkled some rice grains from the altar into my palms.

"After prayer," he said, tossing my hands toward the ceiling, "we throw."

He explained that the lama performed this ritual every morning and evening to bless the earth and his soul, ensuring the fertility of each. *What a beautiful way to end each day.* I wished I had traditions like this. In Christianity, we are supposed to communicate with God through the Holy Spirit, who lives inside you. Protestants denounce ritualistic prayers as empty and meaningless. We are supposed to pray from the heart. We certainly don't have any ritual prayers to bless the earth.

At dinner that night, the lama's wife handed me a bowl of noodles and greens. *Top Ramen.* Gazing at the bowl, I realized that all this time I'd been eating Top Ramen, not traditional Sherpa food. *They must think this is Western food.* I watched the lama's wife ladle out bowls of rich Sherpa stew with chunks of meat and potatoes. *Why aren't I allowed to eat the same food as everyone else?* Dinner was a silent affair. Besides the lama and

Gandji, there were two other women and the granddaughter. No one spoke. I tried not to stare as the women ate deftly with their fingers, scooping up the sauce by cupping their first two fingers and licking them clean. Gandji and the lama used spoons. They ignored the women.

After dinner, Gandji held up a pack of playing cards. The lama's face lit up. An animated debate followed. The lama's wife pursed her lips and shook her head. *Is this a gambling game?* The lama poured a clear liquid into two small shot glasses while Gandji dealt the cards. The lama's wife patted my head and motioned toward the fire. I sat on the floor and watched. Apparently, the game was good entertainment.

I tried to follow the rules. Gandji drew first and threw his cards down with a flourish. The lama shook his head, frowning, as though his cards were bad. Then he threw down two cards and roared with laughter. He had won.

Gandji and the lama were just beginning a second round when the door rattled and two Sherpas from the French expedition entered. They smiled and blew on their hands. I recognized the young man from the campfire. He grinned at me. Gandji said something and everyone laughed. *How did they know we were here?*

The lama's wife ladled out stew, while the lama pulled up more chairs. They played another round, then another. More Sherpas arrived. Some joined, but some stood around the table with their arms crossed. Money appeared. The air grew tense. The Sherpas murmured and shook their heads. The game went on and on. Every time someone dealt cards, they did it with a loud thwack, slamming the deck down as hard as they could. The onlookers shook their heads while the players drank more clear liquid and threw down more money. The stakes were high.

After a couple of hours, the lama's wife rose, shaking her head and *tsking* to herself. I wanted to stay. The young Sherpa was still there, but it was late. Waves of sleep washed over me. I realized the other women had already left. Maybe I should go too. As I turned to leave, the Sherpa winked at me. *What does a wink mean here? Is it the same as back home?* I smiled and hurried to the shrine room.

As I drifted off to sleep, the voices from the adjoining room grew louder and more animated. I recognized the lama's loud laugh. After what seemed like hours, I heard him bid everyone goodbye. He sounded pleased. Gandji came in, pulled his blankets up, and promptly fell asleep. *How much money did he lose?*

Smoke curled into shapes and hung suspended in the sunlight. The smell of scorched herbs filled the room. Squinting from my sleeping bag, I watched the lama fill the water bowls. He worked from left to right, carefully wiping each bowl clean before tipping water from one bowl to the other. I lay still, listening to the chanting.

"*Om namo bhagavate bendzay sarwaparma dana . . .*" His voice rose and fell in the stillness.

I glanced toward Gandji's sleeping bag, but he was gone. I sat up, smoothing my hair with my fingers. It felt like a Brillo pad. I hadn't showered in days. *What do I look like?* A small mirror by the altar caught my eye. When the lama left, I tiptoed across the room.

The girl in the reflection looked strange. Blue eyes stared out from a deeply tanned face. Her dirty-blond hair lay matted around her cheeks. The cheekbones appeared more pronounced—firmer, as though she knew something she hadn't known before. I smiled. I had lost weight.

Outside, Gandji talked to the lama. I could smell fried bread wafting from the kitchen. I pulled on my dress, shoved my feet into my boots, and walked out.

Gandji shot me a rueful grin. "I lose." He pointed to his pocket to show he had no money.

"I see," I said.

"Gambling no good for Sherpa." He laughed.

The lama's wife came out with a steaming pot and handed me a cracked teacup. I sipped butter tea. Butter tea is made from black tea, butter, and salt. In high altitudes, it replaces salt and adds fat to the local diet. Today, it tasted more like chicken broth, only slightly rancid.

Gandji pointed at the blue sky and smiled. I smiled back. We made exaggerated gestures toward the mountains, the trail, the view. Because I didn't speak the language, people treated me like a child. They patted my head. They pointed to where I should sit, where I should sleep, and what I should eat. They talked around me, as though I didn't exist. Sometimes it felt as if they'd forgotten I was there. I felt like a voyeur, silently peering into their lives, taking notes in my journal, and then moving on.

The lama slapped Gandji on the back and roared with laughter. Gandji shrugged and said something that made them laugh even harder. Then he turned to me and picked up my pack. It was time to go.

"Namaste." I bowed my head to the lama and his wife.

"Namaste." The lama's wife clasped my hands together and leaned in. She said something I didn't understand and waved her hands earnestly. Chuckling, Gandji nodded and kissed her cheek.

As we started down the trail, Gandji stuck out his tongue and rolled his eyes, mimicking a monster. "Yeti."

"Yeti?" I must have looked alarmed because Gandji grinned and nodded vigorously.

"Miche!" He said the word in Sherpa—*man bear.* "But *miche* bad. Bad luck. Bad accident. Death."

"What do we do if we run into one?" I laughed. *Is he joking or serious?*

"Run!" He slapped me on the back, moving in front of me.

I fell into step behind him. I had read about yetis. In one of the most famous accounts, Tenzing Norgay, who summited Mount Everest with Edmund Hillary, described seeing dung on glaciers that were too high for animals. Twice, he found footprints above fifteen thousand feet. Yetis were pictured all over the Himalayas in monastery murals. In these paintings, the yeti is depicted as a two-legged ape with long white hair and stooped shoulders.

As we walked through the forest, I imagined a yeti at every turn. It was midfall. Highland oak and maple grew close together. A carpet of red and yellow leaves covered the ground. Sunlight dappled the forest floor. Trees shifted and groaned in the wind.

By late afternoon, we left the forest and found ourselves on a high windswept pass. I shivered in a cold that blew from the north. The air smelled like snow. Tiny purple flowers bloomed in a carpet of silvery grass. Here and there, dwarflike shrubs grew bent and twisted. My stomach cramped. I felt hot and cold. Waves of lightheadedness left me dizzy. *What's wrong with me?* As if he could read my mind, Gandji stopped and touched my shoulder. He pointed. Ahead, I saw a round hut made from straw bales. A herd of yaks grazed nearby.

"Tea?"

"Yes." I sighed.

A man wearing a stocking cap and leather pants came out to greet us. Deep lines around his eyes crinkled when he smiled.

"Namaste." He waved us in.

Inside, a fire burned from a scooped-out hole in the ground. The heat was intoxicating. I squatted close to the fire and held out my hands. The man placed a black kettle on the coals. He glanced at me.

"Butter tea." Gandji pointed at the kettle. "Or yak?"

The man scooped a small pot of thick, creamy milk from a

bucket near the door—yak's milk.

"Milk, please," I said. As much as I wanted to like butter tea, I just couldn't drink it.

The hut was built from hay bales supported by a frame of sticks. A bed of animal skins and wool rugs covered half the room. In the corner lay stacks of thick cloth.

"What are those?" I asked.

The man pulled a cloak from the pile and hung it up. It was thick and made from wool. It had a hood. Maybe he was a trader. I'd seen Tibetan men wearing these types of cloaks atop their ponies. He pointed vaguely toward the door, mimicking a horse. *Is the man Tibetan?* He had high cheekbones and turquoise studs in his ears. Around his neck, he wore an amulet with feathers.

Through our limited conversation, I gathered that the herder had been here all summer. Soon, he would return to the lower country for the winter. Maybe those cloaks were for trading. Communicating was exhausting. We fell into a comfortable silence, and I stared into the flames.

When the milk boiled, the man handed me the steaming bowl. It tasted thick and sweet. I sipped. Nothing in the world was as wonderful as yak's milk and a warm fire. Just then, a gray cat slipped inside and crouched next to me. I stroked her silky ears and scratched her stomach. The yak herder and Gandji spoke quietly. There was something peaceful about them. Maybe it was my Western perspective, but they seemed to have quieter minds than me, with their laughter and the ease with which they moved and spoke. *Where does their peace come from? Why are they so content?* I wished I could stay there. I wished I was a yak herder. Outside, the wind raced mercilessly down the mountainside. The canvas ceiling shuddered and creaked.

Too soon, it was time to go. The yak herder followed us outside. We bowed and shook hands. He waved as we walked away. About a hundred yards down the trail, I looked back. I could see his small figure, hunched over in the wind. He was still waving.

As we descended into the windswept valley, the trail looped around boarded-up shacks where herders would spend the cold winter months. I wondered if the lama and his family from Ngor monastery moved farther down the mountain during the winter too. I remembered the term for this subsistence pattern from anthropology class: *transhumance*, the seasonal migration from lower to higher pastures depending on the season. Here, the practice seemed natural, a way of life. The grassy hillside disappeared, and soon tall pines surrounded us. Under our feet, the trail changed. No longer small, it now expanded into a well-worn path.

"Junbesi." Gandji pointed to a village about half a mile below. The village, with about a hundred homes, looked bigger than the other villages. All were several stories with whitewashed siding and backyard gardens. One building with a fence had children running through the yard, shouting and laughing. *A school maybe?* As we walked, I read off the guesthouse names—Sherpa Inn, Junbesi Retreat (spelled Retreet), and Apple Garden Guesthouse. My stomach tightened. Civilization.

We stopped at the first guesthouse. A burst of laughter spilled from the courtyard. I recognized English voices. Were they Americans or British? After three days of silence and only the soft murmur of Sherpa and Tibetan voices, the sound made me cringe.

We stepped into the courtyard. A group of trekkers sat around a picnic table, drinking beer. They wore Gore-Tex jackets and expensive-looking sunglasses. I glanced down at my red dress and worn-out hiking boots. My Bohemian-anthropologist style helped me fit in with the Sherpas at Ngor lamasery; but in front of these trekkers, I felt ridiculous.

"Hello." I tried to smile.

"Hullo," the trekkers said together.

So, they're British. It bothered me that I couldn't see their eyes behind their reflective sunglasses.

"Nice afternoon, isn't it?" I shaded my eyes from the bright sun.

One of the men nodded. "Yes, bloody hot earlier."

I stood there, expecting more, but the group remained silent. I wanted to crawl into a hole. I felt like a freak. "Enjoy your beer," I said, hurrying inside to ask about a room.

I didn't mind traveling alone, but I didn't like the way people looked at me. *Do they feel obligated to talk to me? Do they think I'm strange? Probably.*

The owner handed us our keys and pointed up the stairs. Our room was on the second floor, simple and clean with two twin beds on either side of a small window. Gandji set my pack near a bed and nodded, a signal that I should mingle with "my own kind." I grabbed my journal and guidebook and headed for the courtyard.

A young girl with light-blond hair and dark-red lips sat off to one side. She was smoking a cigarette and drinking a Diet Coke. I smiled and nodded at her. She watched me for a few minutes before walking over.

"You're alone?" she asked.

"Yes."

"Me too." The girl took a long drag. "I'm Anita . . . from London."

Anita-from-London was possibly the most beautiful girl I had ever seen. Her arching, pencil-thin eyebrows and wide blue eyes fascinated me. She had trekked to Everest Base Camp with friends a few weeks ago. But her friends had flown back to Kathmandu, leaving her alone. Now, she was with people she'd met along the way.

Anita glanced at Gandji. "How much are you paying your porter?"

"He's not my porter," I said. "He's my guide."

Anita scrunched her nose and frowned. "Bloody porters.

They call themselves guides to gyp you out of more money."

Gandji stared down at his tennis shoes, refusing to look at us. I felt my cheeks flush. *Can he understand our conversation?*

"I suppose so," I said.

Anita launched into a long narrative about her adventures. She told me how she was ill and nursed by a wonderful Frenchman named Julian. Julian stayed with her every night. He brought her hot water bottles and broth. Julian was a mountaineer from the French Alps.

As we talked, an entourage of young, bearded trekkers milled through the courtyard. Anita seemed to know all of them. I supposed there were many Julians, eager to help her out.

"Where's your room?" Anita asked suddenly. "He's not sleeping with you, is he?" She pointed at Gandji, as though he were a servant.

"Yes." I shrugged.

Anita pursed her lips. "You'll sleep in *my* room tonight."

I nodded, stealing another peek in Gandji's direction. He studied the ground. I cringed, ashamed of my new association with Anita. I was betraying him. The unspoken friendship we shared for the past two days was suddenly gone, buried beneath the social boundaries of race and gender that didn't seem to matter an hour ago.

That night, I lay in my sleeping bag, listening to Anita's laughter, interspersed with male voices. They must have been in the dining room below. Outside, moonlight covered the hills. Stars glittered overhead. Dogs barked, and right next door a baby cried.

CHAPTER TEN

◁❘▢◉❘▢❘◉❘◉❘◉❘▢❘◉◻❘▷

THE NEXT MORNING, GANDJI'S pack was gone. He had left without saying goodbye. I stared at the empty beds.

Why did I treat him like that?

Suddenly, I hated Anita. And I hated myself for going along with her. I didn't want to be here anymore. Stepping outside, the gray sky made me feel even more depressed. My breath froze as soon as it hit the air.

What am I doing here? Who am I kidding? I'm not an anthropologist. I'm not a mountaineer. I'm just a naïve, stupid girl. Stupid and ugly. Ugly, ugly, ugly. Today, I'll fast the whole day. I won't eat anything.

In the courtyard, two gray kittens chased each other across the cobblestones where the trekkers and Anita were busy, preparing to leave. I sat at the picnic table and sipped a cup of tea. I felt torn. I didn't want to keep trekking, but I didn't want to stay here alone.

"Are you going on?" Anita stooped and picked up her pack.

"I don't know. Maybe I'll take a rest day." In reality, I wanted to go back to bed.

"You should visit the monastery," one of the bearded trekkers said as he tied his boots.

"Where's that?"

"Up there." He motioned with his water bottle. "It's the largest monastery outside Tengboche."

I squinted in the direction he pointed. I could barely make out a roof of one of the buildings. Tiny, maroon-robed figures climbed up and down the steep trail that led to the monastery.

"Did you go there?" Anita asked the trekker.

"No, but another guy did. He said it was cool. There are nuns there too."

I fiddled with my teacup. "That sounds neat."

"Be well," Anita said, suddenly sweet. She gave me an airy kiss on the cheek.

"Yeah, safe travels to you too." I watched as they walked away. Anita took the lead. The British guys followed her, probably because they wanted to watch her walk with her slim, Lycra-covered body.

Maybe I should visit the monastery. A sharp wind whipped through my hair. It was going to snow soon. I shivered. I was unbelievably lonely.

I stepped inside the guesthouse. A small boy with wild hair and a rakish grin squatted over a tub of dishes. *"Tato pani!"* He pointed to a kettle of boiling water.

"Ah," I said. "Hot water?"

My statement delighted him. He followed me around, pointing out various items while I repeated them in English. I learned the words for soap, socks, house, stick, cat, kitten, boy, and many others. The game went on and on. At last, desperate to get away, I gathered my notebook and headed out for Thupten Choling. It was time to visit the nuns.

About six months ago, I started corresponding with a Carmelite nun from Oregon. Monasticism fascinated me. I read works from the early mystics like Teresa of Ávila, Hildegard of Binghen, and the Swedish saint Birgitta. Although their descriptions of Jesus and divine ecstasy made me uncomfortable, I liked the idea of giving my life to a greater cause. Without Christianity, I felt directionless. Lost.

Do Tibetan nuns feel a spiritual calling? Or is their commitment a way to get out of life's daily drudgery, such as raising children or farming?

I wanted to find out. The monastery was perched precariously on a high hill overlooking the valley. Behind the white walls and fluttering prayer flags, forested slopes rose on all sides. White peaks towered in the distance.

As I walked, shaggy Tibetan dogs snarled from their leashes. Donkeys brayed and chickens scratched. Women with jerry cans on their heads paused to greet me. A pack of mules with bundles and bells hurried behind me. Their hooves thudded against the packed dirt. The mule driver, a short, weathered-looking man wearing a baseball cap, flicked his whip, just missing their ears. Bounding up the trail, their brown eyes sparkled. I ran to stay ahead of them.

Cresting the hill, the ground leveled out. I found myself standing outside a large courtyard. *Am I allowed to go in?* When the mule caravan arrived, a man in a yellow robe ran out to greet them. He waved to the mule driver, and they all stepped inside. I followed.

White-washed buildings with rows upon rows of windows surrounded the main courtyard. The lower walls were painted with bright Buddhist murals. Grinning gods and Buddha incarnations peered down at me as I stood, shivering in the weak sunlight.

As the monks helped unload the caravan, their maroon robes flapped in the wind. Prayer beads swung from their necks. In the corner of the courtyard sat a group of nuns, sorting potatoes. They had short, cropped hair and gentle faces. They laughed and talked quietly among themselves. I watched as they tossed potatoes into different piles.

What would it be like to have no hair? They all look identical, almost boyish. If I were a nun, I probably wouldn't care about being desirable. Beauty wouldn't matter anymore.

One of the nuns waved at me. When she smiled, deep creases around her eyes darkened. She had no teeth. Handing me a potato, she patted the ground. Everyone fell quiet as they stared at me. I tossed the potato into a pile. They laughed. It took me a while to catch onto their system. First, I had to peel the eyes off. The larger ones went into one pile and the smaller, to another. Split or rotten potatoes were tossed into a pile for seed.

The afternoon sun felt warm. When we finished filling a basket, monks brought out a new one. The monks shoveled the sorted potatoes into gunny sacks and carted them away. The baskets seemed endless, but the hours flew by. I felt happy. I enjoyed working with the nuns. It was peaceful, listening to their voices rise and fall.

Suddenly, I realized everyone was looking at me. A younger woman sitting across from me had asked a question. She repeated it. The old woman on my right shrugged and touched my hair. She said something I didn't understand. Then she made cutting motions with her fingers.

The younger woman leaned forward. "You cut!" She waved a pair of rusty shears at me.

I laughed and shook my head, but I was curious. *Could I lose myself here and never return?* I imagined the long afternoons, learning Tibetan, working in the gardens, and climbing up and down the steep trails. I fantasized about wearing maroon robes, wandering in the mountains, praying, and chanting. *What would it be like to devote myself to nonstriving, simplicity, and devotion to others? What would my parents say?* I felt drawn to this type of life.

Years before, one Christmas Eve when I was still living at home, my self-imposed starving came to a sudden halt. I had become quiet and withdrawn, spending evenings locked in my room practicing ballet. At that time, I weighed eighty-nine pounds. That night, my father watched me from across the table. When I stood and walked to the sink, he intercepted me. He grabbed the Tupperware cup before I could empty it down the garbage disposal and he stared at me, incredulous.

"What is this?"

Christmas music played in the background. Extended family chattered around the dinner table. I stood frozen.

His face whitened as he squeezed his eyes shut for a second. "We'll talk later." His voice crumbled.

I gazed at my feet. I couldn't meet his eyes. That night was terrible.

"I don't understand," Mom kept saying over and over.

"You're going to stop this!" Dad said, as if he believed he could still control things the way he used to.

I said nothing. Outside, snow fell thick and fast. I could see it under the garage light, piling into drifts. Inside, I felt empty. No fear, no worry, no nothing.

After that night, my parents continuously lectured me about food and my health. I lied and pretended to eat. They sent me to a church counselor. He sat behind his desk and frowned. His shoulders slouched. Neither of us wanted to be there. He kept asking questions, but I said nothing.

One day, I found a brochure on my bed. As I picked it up, my stomach sank. It was for a psychiatric hospital that specialized in eating disorders. That scared me.

"Are you crazy?" I asked my mom. "I'm not even that thin. I'm fine."

I didn't end up going to the hospital. That spring, my dad helped me find my first job waiting tables. Maybe he thought if I kept busy, I'd quit obsessing about my weight. It worked. I was so busy working double shifts that after a while, food—or the lack of it—became less important. Living with anorexia sometimes felt like another presence lived inside me. Working and talking to people all day, every day, the need to not eat quieted, almost as if I had tamed it somehow. Life went back to normal.

But something in me had changed. Somewhere in between starving and feeling empty, I felt something else—something that was all mine, and not my parents', or sister's, or the church's. It was a silence. A way of being empty and full at the same time. When I didn't eat, I felt suspended between my body and my spirit. It was almost like meditation—a deep, invincible peace. I felt it first as I learned to fall asleep hungry—and later, on my long runs in the hills. After miles and miles of open grass meadows and meandering dirt roads, I felt peace.

When I got my driver's license, I started hiking alone. In those alpine meadows and high peaks, I felt a presence, something that was part of me but older at the same time. It felt like the Hindus' description of the atman, the universal soul. Some part of me was eternal, timeless. Not eating tapped into that presence, but being in the mountains made it come alive. This was the beginning of my own spirituality.

I felt that same presence kneeling on the floor, looking into the Buddha's face. It was as if I had finally come home. *Perhaps this is what I am supposed to do with my life.* I stared at the nun who held the cutting shears. *Become a nun? Could I stay here forever?*

Although I knew that the thought was a passing fantasy, the notion lodged somewhere inside my chest, always a tiny spark of possibility.

After we sorted potatoes, I followed one of the nuns to the kitchen, where an elderly monk bent over a huge black cauldron.

He stirred the bubbling contents with a long paddle. I sniffed. Butter tea. The man motioned for me to sit. I glanced around. There were no benches or chairs, just piles and piles of supplies. Bags of rice, crates of tea, and packages of powdered orange Tang. I sat on a bag of rice and smiled.

A boyish-looking monk appeared in the doorway with the mule driver behind him.

"Hello." The mule driver nodded at me.

He just spoke English. I waited until he found a seat. "You speak English?"

"Yes." A cheerful man in his mid-thirties, he wore a little felted hat and a woolen vest. He seemed to know both monks. Maybe he came here often.

"How old is this monastery?" I asked.

"Thirty years. Is not that old." He explained that during the Cultural Revolution many Tibetans escaped over the mountains, settling here in Junbesi. Eventually, his holiness Trulsik Rinpoche built a monastery for the refugees.

The elderly monk handed me a cup of tea. I took a sip. "How many monks and nuns live here?"

"Ah . . ." The mule driver hummed. "Many, many. Maybe six hundred? Seven hundred?" He chuckled. "Tibetan. All speak Tibetan. Sherpas." He pointed at himself and shook his head. "We do not understand."

The younger monk piped in and said something to the mule driver, which he relayed back to me.

It seemed that today was a special day because two holy priests were coming from Tengboche. Just that morning, a group of Japanese Buddhists had arrived with gifts of food and supplies. This explained the mule caravan and the mess in the kitchen.

"Still unpacking." The mule driver pointed to the crates and bags littered across the kitchen.

"Is that common?" I asked. "To receive gifts like this?"

"Yes, yes." The mule driver nodded. "Thupten Choling live off gifts from abroad. Lots of foreigners." He glanced at the younger monk, who rifled through one of the boxes. The monk handed me a bottle.

"He wants to know what it's for," the mule driver said.

I turned it over in my hand—vitamin C pills. "It's for health," I said. "Fighting colds and flus."

"How many?" the mule driver asked, still interpreting.

"One a day," I replied.

The monk seemed pleased with the information. He said something to the mule driver.

"He wants to know if you're a doctor."

"No, not at all." I laughed. Sipping my tea, I glanced out the window.

Several monks were crossing the courtyard carrying large trays of colorful sculptures made from butter. I'd always wanted to see these sculptures for myself. They were molded from dyed butter and shaped into different Buddhist deities. Tibetans use them in special ceremonies as offerings. After the ceremony, they destroy the sculptures to reflect the impermanence of all things.

The young monk said something about prostrations. He showed me how to do it. Bend at the waist. Kneel to your knees. Press your forehead against the ground and then stand.

"Self-discipline," he said.

Prostrations developed self-discipline and brought one closer to enlightenment. Similar to reciting prayers and meditation, prostration was a form of self-purification.

The young monk sighed and glanced out the window.

The mule driver cleared his throat. "His greatest desire is to perform prostrations around Mount Kailas, in Tibet. You know Kailas?"

"Yes, I've heard of it," I said.

Prostrations always reminded me of ballet—the endless, repetitive folding, bending, and extending. But prostrations were not about sculpting the body. They were about self-purification, losing oneself, and becoming one with the Buddha nature. *Is that what I've been doing all along? Ballet as a form of self-purification? Fasting? Maybe Buddhism is what I've been looking for. What if I really could convert? I could do it. I could become a Buddhist nun. Maybe I would find the peace I crave.*

When I stood to leave, it was almost dark.

The young monk clasped my hand and bowed low. *"Namaste."* He touched his forehead with his hand.

I bowed. *"Namaste." Will I ever see him again?*

As I walked through the courtyard, a group of monks hurried out of the monastery, carrying scarves. The white silks billowed in the wind. Near the entrance stood two older men with white beards that fell past their waists. Their tall, pointed hats reminded me of a fairy tale. The monks prostrated themselves before the elderly men, who nodded and bowed. They must have been the priests from Tengboche.

No one noticed me as I slipped through the entrance and headed down the trail. A full moon illuminated the landscape. Trees rustled in the cool breeze. White stupas with their Buddha eyes glowed in the moonlight. I hurried, hoping I would remember how to get to my guesthouse. I felt less lonely than I did this morning. My mind churned with the images of the nuns, the sound of their laughter, and the priests with their long beards.

Later, in my sleeping bag, I watched the moon and allowed my mind to wander. When I drifted off to sleep, I dreamed of my mother. We were shopping for a red dress.

"I need to find one," she kept saying. "I need to find a red dress!"

"Okay, Mom. We'll find one."

All night, the two of us searched in strange cities and countries. We never did find that red dress.

CHAPTER ELEVEN

◁I▢◉I▢I◉I◉I◉I▢I◉◁I▷

THE TRAIL FROM JUNBESI to Ringmo led through rolling hills dotted with apple trees and forests carpeted with yellow leaves. As I walked, I smelled woodsmoke and the sweet, sharp scent of fallen leaves. This made me homesick. *What am I doing out here?* I was five days and a thirteen-hour bus ride from Kathmandu. I had lived on apples and butter tea for the past several days. Now, I felt weak and depressed.

Ringmo was more of a settlement than a village. A few houses clung to the mountainside a thousand feet shy of the pass. Oak and fir trees crowded the meager clearing where a vegetable garden grew thick with weeds. I followed a sign along the trail that read, "Guesthouse Ringmo." As I walked up to the sagging three-story house, a small child wearing a shirt that barely covered his round belly darted away from me. I peered inside and knocked on the doorframe.

"Hello?"

"*Namaste.*" A man in his mid-forties stepped out of the darkness.

"You have a room?"

"Yes." The man led me upstairs to a long dormitory-style room with enough beds for twenty trekkers. I looked around. I was the only one there.

"Excuse me." I hesitated, wondering if he spoke English. "Jirel? Are there Jirel people here?"

He frowned and shook his head. "No Jirel."

I tried again. "Jirel people. Do they live here?"

"I am a Rai. No Jirel." He thumped one of the dirty mattresses with his fist. "Sleep here."

A loud crash echoed up through the narrow stairway. A child cried. The man hurried away, leaving me alone. I dragged my pack to the bed and stared out the window. It was still early afternoon, but the air felt colder. Clouds clung to the mountaintops. The people in Jiri were right—there were no Jirels here. I should have listened to them.

Glancing around, I shivered. The room smelled musty, like mice. I ran my finger along the windowsill. Dust. I sunk onto a narrow mattress and put my face in my hands. I missed my mom. *What would she do if she were me?* I tried to imagine her here in the Himalayas. No. She would never go to a strange country by herself. Thinking about her almost made her seem real. I could sense her lilac perfume and hear her voice.

My parents had moved to Hawaii earlier that year. It was my mother's idea, mostly. I didn't blame her. Her life had revolved around me and my sister. Hawaii was her attempt to deal with us leaving the nest. She needed to go. But still, I felt abandoned.

A mother and daughter chimpanzee remain together for life. Their bond forms the basis of a chimpanzee social group. The Mosuo people in China, who live in matriarchal societies, raise their children with their mothers and grandmothers. Men come and go, but the mother-daughter bond continues forever. I knew I was supposed to be grown up and independent, but without my mother in my life, I was lost.

Alone, in Seattle, I'd had a crisis. The girls next door had blared their music from early morning to late at night. I couldn't study or concentrate. I couldn't sleep. I'd lay awake with my hand on the wall, feeling the vibration from the speakers. I spoke to the resident advisor on duty. She laughed and suggested earplugs. After a week of not sleeping, I had to move. I found a moldy basement apartment about an hour's walk from campus. I didn't know if I could afford it. I had a work study job at the library, and I cleaned houses once a week. Once tuition and rent were paid, I had twenty dollars left. Every payday, with that twenty dollars, I bought one bagel with cream cheese. I ate it slowly, savoring the soft, creamy flavor and the doughy onion bread. I filled my car with gas and purchased eggs, butter, milk, and coffee. I cut the butter into tiny slices, so it would last a week. One slice per day. No more.

When my sister came to visit, my empty refrigerator horrified her. "Is this all you have to eat?"

I shrugged.

"Let's go shopping." To my chagrin, she charged groceries to her credit card.

In my family, we took great pride in being self-sufficient. Admitting that I was in trouble was unacceptable. Asking my parents for money was not an option. They were three thousand miles away. Why didn't my mother know I needed her help? Did she even care about me? I walked to campus to save money—an hour a day, back and forth. Sometimes I was so hungry when I returned, I couldn't sleep.

One day, a few students took me dumpster diving. "You live next to that fancy bakery in Greenwood and you don't know about their dumpster?" Late at night, we climbed a chain-link fence behind the bakery. The dumpster was about ten feet high. I had to stand on someone's shoulders and lean over to reach the bread. I returned home with a couple of slightly stale loaves of sundried tomato and kalamata olive bread.

I lived on bread and coffee for the rest of the year. I never told my parents about dumpster diving or that I needed money.

Something about not having food made me feel powerful and stoic.

Now, sitting on the dirty bed in the Himalayas, I didn't feel powerful. I was miserable. I was lonely. I glanced around. Another staircase caught my attention. Tiptoeing up the stairs, I found a small storage room. Sheaves of wheat and piles of apples and potatoes covered the floor. I crouched next to a window that looked out over the valley. Outside, the wind whistled through the trees as the rain fell. From somewhere, a toddler screamed. My stomach hurt. My throat swelled, and my eyes filled with tears. I hated being alone. I just wanted to go home.

I heard my mother's voice as if she were sitting next to me. *Julie, what are you doing out here all by yourself?* I could picture her in the red dress she wore years ago. It was cotton with spaghetti straps. *What's wrong, honey?*

"I don't know, Mom. I don't know what I'm doing here. I'm scared and I'm sick. Why didn't you help me when I needed you?" Hot tears ran down my face. I wasn't the independent girl I wanted to be. "I want to go back."

Back to where, honey?

"Back to you. Back to our life before everything changed."

When my sister, Jennifer, rebelled, my parents were devastated. "We should never have had kids," my dad had said, shaking his head.

I stood there wondering, *What about me? Do they wish they didn't have me too?* That's when I vowed I would never be a burden to anyone again. I'd make my own money, pay for my own college, and then, one day, go far away from home. It would be as if they'd never had me.

Sitting by the window in the storage room, I cried. *Why didn't you want me, Mom? Why? I did everything to make things better between you, Dad, and Jennifer. Why wasn't I enough?* Outside, the rain poured and wind rattled the walls. I cried until there were no tears left. My mind grew quiet.

Again, my mother's voice: *Julie, I love you. You know how much I love you. See? Even when I'm not with you, my love is.*

Silence.

My love is always with you. Always.

I imagined her presence. I could feel it.

Even someday when I'm gone, honey, my love will be with you.

"Okay, Mom," I whispered into the stillness.

Why don't you see if you can have someone make you a cup of tea? Or read a book. You'll feel much better.

I sniffled. The idea of some hot tea did sound nice. Maybe I could read in my sleeping bag.

Why don't you see if they have lemon tea? my mother said.

Lemon tea. That was a good idea.

I walked down the stairs and asked the man for some tea. He had a kettle on the fire.

"Yes, yes." He waved.

I went back upstairs and crawled into my sleeping bag.

A couple of hours later, a loud, breathless young man burst through the door.

"Hello there!" he said in a Kiwi accent. Without waiting for a response, he threw his pack in the corner and flopped down on a bed near mine, panting. "Thought I'd never make it."

"Where did you come from?" I felt silly huddled in my sleeping bag. I hoped he couldn't tell I'd been crying.

"Gorakh Shep, ten hours today. I almost didn't make it, swear to God."

"What's your name?"

"Chris. From New Zealand." He grinned.

Chris-from-New Zealand shaved his head. He had ruddy cheeks and a loud, but not unpleasant, laugh. Maybe twenty-five years old or so? That seemed old to me. We exchanged the familiar where-have-you-been, where-are-you-going. He had trekked to Everest Base Camp and Gokyo Lakes. Now, he was hiking out to Jiri.

Crossing his arms behind his head, Chris launched into a story. "It was crazy, mate. This bloke was up at Gorek Shep. It's a bloody five thousand meters, you know. And he's got a headache, but he won't go back down, right?"

I nodded.

Chris paused and unlaced his trekking boots. "Phew, ripe!" He ducked out and placed the offending boots in the hallway. "Anyway, so the bloke has a headache, and his mates put him to bed. In the morning, they go over and phht." He blew air through his lips. "That's it. He's dead." Chris peeled off his outer shirt before rummaging through his pack.

"Really?" Suddenly, I felt more cheerful.

"Oh, mate, it's crazy up there. Past Lukla, the scene's intense. Tons of people, porters, guides, expeditions, expensive gear. Down here is more like I thought trekking would be." He paused and glanced at me. "So, where you headed, mate?"

I told him I was conducting ethnographic fieldwork with the Jirels but had lost my way and had taken a detour.

"You're not trekking then?"

"Not really."

"Huh." He smiled. "Well, you'd better come out with me in the morning. I have to be in Kathmandu by the twenty-ninth to meet up with my mates. We're doing karaoke at the Blue Note Bar. You should join us."

"I'll see," I said. Given my miserable afternoon, maybe company would be nice.

Chris and I played cards while we waited for our meal. Children ran in and out, screaming and pushing each other. Every so often, they'd stop and stare at us, then laugh and point, before darting back out.

"It'd be rough," Chris said.

"What would?"

"Living up here; all these mouths to feed."

The man sat our food on the table. He looked exhausted. *Where is his wife? Maybe she died.*

After dinner, we found a pile of children's schoolbooks in our room. We skimmed through them until dark. Noise from the family getting ready for bed drifted up the stairs. A child cried, and the man yelled. Chris placed his sleeping bag out on the bunk next to mine.

"If you get cold, mate, there's plenty of room in here." He casually patted his bag. A gold stud in his tongue glinted in the moonlight.

"I think I'll be okay." *Should I be afraid of this guy with a tongue stud?*

"Good night then, sweetheart. Chris rolled over and tucked his arms under his head.

I waited for him to say something else, but he didn't. In a few moments, I heard snoring. Relieved, I snuggled deeper into my bag. I wasn't afraid of him. In fact, I was glad he was there. Tomorrow, maybe I would hike out with him, back to Jiri.

CHAPTER TWELVE

⊲❑❙❑◉❙❑❙◉❙◉❙◉❙❑❙◉❑❙▷

"HIYA," CHRIS SAID FROM across the room.

I rolled over and tried to open my eyes. *Where am I?*

Chris was stuffing his sleeping bag into his pack. He smiled at me. "Rise and shine, sweetheart."

"Umm." It all came flooding back; Nepal, trekking, Chris. A crash echoed from somewhere below, and a toddler wailed.

"Meet you downstairs?" Chris patted his pack.

"Sure." I smoothed out my hair and forced a smile. I hated seeing strangers first thing in the morning. I jumped up and fumbled for my clothes. Outside, the sky looked cold and gray. I shivered. I couldn't wait to get out of there.

Downstairs, Chris was leaning over the fire, warming his hands.

"Namaste." The father handed me a cup of tea, then flipped a chapati with his fingers. The skillet sizzled over the hot flames.

"Ah!" Laughing, one of the children plucked a dead rat from a bucket of water near the door. The father threw it outside. I cringed. *Is that the water our tea came from?*

The father ignored the child and the rat and continued with his cooking. Chris and I glanced at each other. I set my tea down. Suddenly, I didn't feel like eating.

We gave the man a hundred rupee note and picked up our packs. We waved goodbye, leaving the handful of settlements clinging to the hillside. After a few steps, I glanced back. The sagging houses looked pitiful against the pristine forest. One of the children watched us leave. He waved. I waved back.

Walking hurt my muscles with each step. Every few yards, I doubled over with stomach cramps. Chris glanced at me and frowned.

"Here." He handed me his water bottle. "Have a drink."

I took a sip. It tasted like iodine. I grimaced.

Noticing my frown, Chris added, "Apple juice? We can get some at the next stop."

"No, I'm fine."

"Candy?" He held out a handful of hard purple treats.

"No, really," I shook my head, "I'm fine."

"Suck on one." He unwrapped one and put it in my hand. "It helps."

"I think I'm sick."

"Yep." Chris shrugged. "Lots of people get sick out here."

We continued up the trail, and I struggled as Chris talked. Distraction was good about now.

"Did I tell you about that hundred-year-old Japanese guy?" Chris asked.

"No, you didn't."

Chris launched into a story about a famous Japanese man who jumped into one of the lakes up at Gokyo. "He had to chop a hole in the ice." Chris laughed. "I guess he'd been doing this every year for something like thirty years. I don't know, but it made international headlines."

"Ahh." I couldn't imagine jumping into a lake at fifteen thousand feet, especially if I was a hundred years old. At fifteen thousand feet, the lakes would be completely frozen over. "Why did he jump?"

"He said it made him live longer. Must have worked."

I laughed.

Later, I learned that Gokyo Lakes were considered sacred to Hindus and Buddhists. They would bathe in the waters every August during an annual festival. Maybe the Japanese man was following that tradition. Chris's supply of stories kept me entertained throughout the morning. But by afternoon, I started to tire.

"I'm sorry," I panted as I climbed a rock where Chris sat. "You should go on; leave me."

"Not on your life, sweetheart." He flicked my stocking cap with his finger.

"I'm slowing you down."

"Nah. I'm in no hurry to get to Kathmandu. Besides," he said, "somebody's gotta look after you."

We continued up the steep mountainside. Low-hanging clouds clung to the slopes. Smoke curled in the air. Women with bright headscarves hurried down with towering loads of firewood on their backs.

By late afternoon, we were exhausted. I told Chris about getting lost and the French group. We also talked about Tibetan Buddhism, yetis, and the Sherpa religion. Chris told me about his year working in London. He described his London flat, his girlfriend, and the parties they threw. All the while, the trail wound up and up. At times, it seemed as though we were walking straight into the cold gray sky. At the top of the pass, we came to a small shack where tea and Cokes were sold.

"Let's stop here," Chris said, glancing at me.

"I'm okay." I tried to smile. I felt a fever coming on. I shivered, and my joints ached. Even my skin hurt to the touch.

"Tea?" Chris took my hand.

The ceiling was low. I had to duck to step inside. Except for one small window, the place was dark. It was no bigger than my living room back home. No wood for the floor, just packed dirt. A rock fireplace no larger than a footstool sat along one wall. A small fire crackled among the large stones. Near a back wall, a stack of Coca-Cola bottles reached up to the mud ceiling. Two older Nepali men sat at a table, smoking cigarettes. A teenage girl silently swept the floor. She watched us intently. A plump older woman, wearing a long-striped apron, nodded at us as we entered.

"Two teas, please." Chris took off his stocking cap and held up two fingers. The woman lifted a large black kettle from the flames. Chris and I found a seat near the fire. It was warm here, but I could feel the wind coming through in the corners. The aged woman hobbled over. Placing the cups in front of us, she gave a toothless smile. I took a sip; English tea, milky and sweet.

The door rattled, and a handsome Nepali woman in her mid-thirties stumbled into the shack. She wore jeans, tennis shoes, and a down coat.

Chris and I smiled. *"Namaste,"* we murmured.

The woman ignored us and turned to the older woman who had made our tea. She shouted out something in Nepali. The older woman shook her head and looked away. The men at the table stared at their feet. The girl sweeping the floor left silently. A cat that had been winding against my leg scattered to a dark corner. Chris and I looked at each other. *What's going on?* Now, the jeans-and-down-coat lady turned to one of the men. Again, she shouted something. The man said nothing. Sighing, he stood and headed for the door. The woman's shoulders sagged. She turned toward the fire and glanced our way.

We looked at our teacups. I studied the thin, cracked china. *Who is this lady?*

"Hello?" I said, wondering if the woman spoke English.

"Hi." She brushed her hand across her face as if to shake off a conflict, and she sighed. "You're American?"

"Yes." I smiled.

"New Zealand," Chris volunteered.

"Ah, a beautiful country, New Zealand. I have heard of it." The woman nodded.

"You're from here?" Chris asked.

"I grew up here. I live in Kathmandu. I am a teacher at an English school." She gave us a weak smile.

Finally, a local who spoke English. I knew I should ask her about the culture, but my head pounded too much to think. I just wanted to lie on the floor and sleep. I tried to think of something intelligent to say, but nothing came to mind aside from the pain.

"Do lots of young people move away to Kathmandu?" This was a really stupid question, but it was all I could think of.

"No, no." The woman shook her head. "Most stay here. I went to secondary school on a scholarship. It's rare, especially for girls. Boys go into the trekking industry, but girls stay."

"You're visiting for a while?" Chris asked.

"Just a few days." The woman frowned. "My father is ill. I am trying to make him go to Kathmandu. He refuses."

"Ah." Chris and I nodded.

"He has a heart condition." The woman patted her chest. "But he doesn't have money for the tests." She fell silent and stared at the fire.

I didn't know what to say. The old woman who poured our tea made a *tsking* sound and touched the younger woman's shoulder. She turned away from us, and the two women started speaking rapidly in Nepali.

Chris looked at me. "Ready?"

I nodded, swallowing the last dregs of the now cold tea. We waved goodbye and ducked before heading out into the cold wind.

I thought about the young woman as I walked. It would be rare for a girl in these parts to get an education. She seemed slightly estranged from her family. Moving up in the world created a barrier between family members. I knew about that. Becoming an anthropologist was like becoming a Martian in my family. *What would my parents say if I told them I was going to become a Buddhist nun?*

The trail spun under my feet. I could feel my temperature rising. It was almost dark when we made it to a guesthouse that perched on the side of the mountain.

"Sete," Chris announced, before disappearing inside. He returned with a key to our room. "This way."

I nodded and followed him up a rickety staircase. Collapsing on a thin mattress, I wanted to cry with relief. I lay still, dimly aware that Chris had unpacked my sleeping bag and was speaking to someone else in the room.

"They're heating water if you want a bucket bath," he said.

A bath sounded wonderful. A few minutes later, a short man with a green stocking cap led me outside to a tiny wooden shack.

"Bath." He opened the door and pointed inside.

A large bucket of steaming water and a bar of soap sat in the middle of a tiny windowless room with cracks in the floor. Nothing had ever looked so inviting. Grateful, I smiled at the man and closed the door. After stripping off my clothes, I scooped cupful after cupful of hot water over my body. I soaped every inch of me and even washed my hair. I ran my hands over my belly and thighs; firm and lean. I was definitely losing weight.

Once back in our room, I crawled into my sleeping bag. Although my head throbbed and I trembled from the fever, it felt wonderful to be clean. Chris ordered us food. I didn't eat. He sat on the open windowsill and finished off his dinner.

"You're sure you don't want any?"

"I'm good." I closed my eyes and dozed.

At some point, I woke to see Chris still sitting in the window. A large yellow moon shone brightly outside. The sharp scent of marijuana filled the air. He was smoking a joint.

"You should eat," Chris said.

"I'm fine." I didn't want to eat, not because I was feeling ill but because I had once again obtained that lovely taste of thinness. I wanted the feeling to stay.

Before I left Seattle Pacific University for Nepal, I had visited my parents in Hawaii. They had moved to Kona, which was on the Big Island. Living on a missionary base called Youth with a Mission, they attended classes on evangelism and missionary work. I had attended missionary schools and churches my whole life. As a child, I went with the flow. Now, however, something had changed. Questioning my religious upbringing, I felt increasingly uncomfortable with structured religion.

I had known since my trip to India that I no longer belonged in the church. In Hawaii, students had sung and danced during worship services. They had prayed with their heads bowed, swaying to the music. I had sat there feeling sick to my stomach. I didn't believe any of it. The realization that I was an imposter hit me like a tidal wave. I panicked. When people asked how long I'd been saved, I couldn't answer. They asked where I was going on my next mission, and I wanted to scream. I was no longer one of them.

During one morning service, several students held long silk banners that signified the River of Life. When the music reached an emotional peak, the students ran through the crowd, waving the banners above their heads. The blue silk fluttered through the crowd, representing the Holy Spirit. Whenever the River of Life appeared, people prayed out loud in tongues and danced in the Spirit.

I watched the banner zigzagging through the air. Someone touched my arm. Evelyn, a friend of my mother's, stood frowning.

Her forehead crinkled with concern. Her wide blue eyes stared directly into mine.

"You seem troubled," she said. "Do you want me to pray for you?"

"Umm." My heart raced. *Can she tell I'm not one of them any longer? Does it show on my face?* "Sure." I didn't want her to pray for me, but at the same time I couldn't say no.

Evelyn led me to a small room. To my surprise, a man and woman were waiting for us. I recognized the man as one of the leaders. He was in his mid-fifties with salt-and-pepper hair and a long, serious face. He leaned forward with his hands folded on his knees. The woman had short gray hair and wore a Hawaiian print dress. They smiled kindly at us.

"Hello. You must be Julie."

How do they know my name? Did my parents ask these people to talk to me? Why do they care about me? Am I in trouble? My heart raced. I felt my cheeks flush. "Hi."

The man cleared his throat. "Evelyn asked us to meet with you. Is there anything you'd like to talk about?" He motioned for me to sit.

I sank into one of the padded folding chairs. "I don't know."

"We'd like you to know that we're here for you. We're ready to answer any question you may have."

Questions? What is he talking about?

Evelyn patted my arm. "Julie, the Spirit is telling me that you have some . . . questions about Christianity." She smiled. "Everyone goes through doubt. It's okay."

The short-haired lady chimed in. "Doubting Thomas had trouble believing. And what did Jesus say to him?"

Ah yes. Doubting Thomas. Thomas who had said, " 'Unless I see the nail marks in his hands and put my finger where the nails were . . .' " I'd always felt sorry for Thomas. Denigrated for two thousand years, he was the one apostle who asked a reasonable

question. I shook my head. "Jesus told Thomas to put his fingers
in the holes of his hands."

"And, he finally believed." The man smiled. "What is it that
you have a hard time believing, Julie?"

My thoughts raced. Tears welled in my eyes. They wouldn't
understand. "I have a hard time with the idea that Christianity
is the only way to God. Sometimes I wonder if Buddhists or
Hindus also know God. I mean, in their own way," I added.

The man ran his fingers through his hair and leaned back.
"Lots of people have wondered about this. Jesus says, *I am the
way, the truth and the life. No one comes to the Father but by
me.* The whole verse is quite clear in the Scripture."

Evelyn nodded. Her eyes narrowed. "That's why we do what
we do here. We're working on the ten-forty window. You would
be interested in this, Julie."

My heart sank. Not again. The ten-forty window is a term
evangelicals use to describe the areas in the world that have
never heard about Christ. It is the band of countries lying ten
degrees north of the equator and forty degrees south. It includes
all the countries like India, Nepal, and West Africa—everywhere
in the world that isn't Christianized.

"We're sending a team to Nepal this year," the short-haired
lady said. "Your parents mentioned you were going to Nepal."

I cleared my throat. "What about Muhammed or the Buddha?
Couldn't their teachings also lead to God?" Even as I said it, I
knew it was the wrong thing to say. The room turned to ice.

"Julie, we know that Muhammed and the Buddha were just
men. They died. Jesus is the Son of God. Those men led people
astray. Don't you want to see the world saved?"

I didn't want to see the world saved. I wanted a chance to
explore it the way it is, in all its beauty and diversity. But I couldn't
say that. These people were my parents' friends. "I suppose so,"
I whispered.

"Let's pray." The man grabbed my hands. The women bowed and placed their hands on my head.

I was such a coward. Why couldn't I stand up for myself? Why couldn't I stand by what I believed?

After that morning, I slipped into a deep depression. I drove to the beach. I sat on the shore and watched the waves crash against the pebbly sand. I felt so alone. I didn't fit within my religion anymore. I didn't fit within my parents' beliefs. Our differences had grown. If I refused to be a Christian, I would always be an outsider to them. And if I didn't belong to them, who *did* I belong to? I was nobody.

I dove into the water and swam through curling, light-filled waves. But everything felt dark. Sea turtles brushed by with their green, gnarled heads bobbing up and down. Their wise eyes blinked at me. I reached out, and a strange, alien flipper grazed my fingertips. They fit in their world. Why couldn't I fit within mine?

CHAPTER THIRTEEN

SLOWLY, MY EYES FOCUSED. My backpack lay open on the bed; books and journals spilled out everywhere. I sat up and looked around. Chris sat across from me, drinking tea.

"Morning." He handed me a steaming cup.

"Thank you." I felt a little better today. At least the fever was gone. My body no longer ached.

"Sleep well?"

"Yes." I sipped the tea. "I think I can hike today."

We ate breakfast outside in the courtyard. The sun shone brightly in a deep-blue sky. Yesterday's winter seemed to have come and gone. From our picnic table, we could see the trail we'd hiked last night. Green forests covered the steep mountainside. Tiny houses and terraced fields dotted the valley far below. I inhaled. The air smelled of pine trees and cooking fires.

Chris spread his map on the table. "Looks like we cross the Kenja River today and then go on to Bhandar." He traced the squiggly line with his finger. "Maybe seven hours? Depending on how steep."

"I stayed in Bhandar on my way in. It's a nice village," I said. I was almost back to where I started. I was sick of traversing the steep trails, sweating on hot days, and freezing during cold nights. I was sick of bucket baths and outhouses and noodles. "Then onto Jiri the next night."

"Yep. Can't wait to get back to Kathmandu."

The thought of Kathmandu made me anxious. *What are Charla and the YWAM team doing? Will they still expect me to chaperone the teens? Where would I go next? How would I study the Jirels from Kathmandu?*

"Shall we go?" I didn't feel like ruminating on my failed research project.

"Let's do it. Gonna be a hot one today."

We left the village of Sete and continued up the mountainside. Birds sang. The air felt warm and dry. My stomach had shrunk, so I'd had to take in my belt a couple of notches. *Thinner, thinner, thinner,* I sang to myself. *How much thinner can I get?*

At the top of the pass we stopped alongside a shack with a sign that read, "Cheese Factory." Ravens cawed in the distance. Prayer flags fluttered in the wind. Chickens clucked along the trail, and every so often a goat wandered by to nibble at the grass.

"Want anything?" Chris asked.

"No, I'm okay." I sat on a stone wall and looked around.

A young man in dress slacks and a white shirt panted up the hill from the opposite direction. I watched him struggle. He wore leather shoes and a small daypack. Sweat dripped down his face. When he reached the courtyard, he threw down his pack and guzzled some water. He glanced at me and frowned. "Your pack's undone."

"Oh." I looked at it. The top hung open. "Thanks." As I fiddled with the stuck zipper, Chris appeared with a hunk of cheese.

"Hiya, mate."

"Hello." The young man brushed dust from the stones before sitting. He removed one of his shoes and shook out a pebble. Then he carefully wiped the shoe with a hanky before putting it back on.

"Where are you headed?" Chris asked.

"A small settlement. Three days up."

"You from here?" Chris sliced off a chunk of cheese and bit into it.

"Yes, my family lives here."

I looked out over the vast expanse of valleys and mountains. In the distance, forested foothills gave way to jagged white peaks. A ring of clouds hung far to the north. Everywhere I turned, mountains shimmered against the horizon. "So beautiful," I said. "I bet you'd never want to leave."

The young man shook his head. "For you, yes. It's beautiful. For us, it's our life." He sighed, wiping the sweat from his brow.

I nodded. *What would it be like to grow up with a dirt floor?* He took great care with his leather shoes. Maybe he didn't have any as a kid. The mountains that I found so enchanting would be an obstacle for local people. No roads. No emergency rooms. No schools. It was prestigious being from the city. People from Kathmandu regarded those from the countryside as backwards and illiterate. I had no idea what it would be like to grow up out here. I felt properly ashamed.

"What'd ya do in Kathmandu?" Chris asked.

"I'm a businessman. I sell shoes." He glared at us.

"Are those the shoes you sell?" I pointed to his feet.

"Yes." He nodded. "My family is Kami. That is our caste. We make shoes. I sell them."

"They're beautiful." I smiled at the man, hoping to win his approval after offending him. "What is the Kami caste?"

"We are leather workers." The young man seemed agitated. He shifted and scratched his head. "I must go," he said, picking up his pack and nodding. He walked down the trail.

"Bye," I said.

Chris and I waved.

The Kami are considered untouchables because they work

with the hide of dead animals. They are one of the lowest castes in Nepal. Maybe the man's defensiveness came from years of discrimination.

"He sure didn't seem to be happy going home," I said.

"Nope." Chris finished his cheese and took a drink from his water bottle. "You ready?"

"Sure." I hoisted my pack onto my shoulder. Taking one last look at the mountains, I headed down the hard-packed trail, leaving the cheese factory and the ravens behind.

As we walked, Chris and I fell into a companionable silence. I was grateful to be walking downhill. Chris seemed lost in his own thoughts. Down, down, down. The trail descended in a series of relentless switchbacks. This was the section I'd gotten lost on last week. Peering down, I saw the outline of a river glinting in the sun. The vegetation grew denser and lusher. Bushes crowded the trail.

By the time we reached the settlement, the sun hung low in the sky. Sweat dripped down the back of my dress. Chris's face was flush.

"I'm going in the river," Chris said, dumping his pack near the rushing water.

"Want a Coke?" I felt like I should repay all the teas and Cokes he'd bought me.

"Sure." He peeled off his T-shirt. "I'll watch your stuff for you."

Shrugging, I let my pack slide onto the sand. I stood for a moment, relishing how light I felt without it. Ahead, several mud-packed buildings lay scattered along the trail. Their red walls were topped with grass-thatched roofs. Round, open windows faced the river. A sign read, "Tea House." Ducking under the low doorframe, I stood for a second, letting my eyes adjust. A small man sat bent over a single table. In the corner sat crates of soda in glass bottles. Cases of eggs and sacks of flour lay stacked along the wall.

"Hello." I smiled hesitantly. "Coke?"

"Yes, *didi*." The man rose and shuffled toward one of the crates.

"Two?" I held up two fingers.

"Sixty rupees." The man handed me the Cokes, and I gave him a crumpled note. "Ah." He held up his hand for me to wait. He fumbled around in his pocket then pulled out a bottle opener and popped the tab on both.

"Namaste." I bowed low. "I'll bring the bottles back." He shook his head. I pretended to drink the Coke, and patted the table. "I'll come back."

"Ah. Is okay." He waved his hand.

I hurried to the river. Chris sat on the bank with his arms slung over his knees. "Thanks, mate."

I sat next to him. We sipped the soda, savoring each sugary mouthful. The sun beat down on our heads. The air smelled musty and wet. Willows and beech trees crowded the banks. A hundred yards downstream, women washed their clothes. They stood in the water with their skirts pulled up to their knees, kneading the material with their hands. White bubbles swirled around them before floating away in the current. I thought of the large bar of soap in my pack. It must have bleach in it. Every night when I washed out my clothes with that soap, it turned everything remarkably clean but slightly faded. It had to be terrible for the environment.

Chris spread out his map. "Looks like another two or three hours to Bhandar." He glanced at me. "You feeling okay?"

"Yeah, pretty good."

"'Cause we could stay here or keep going."

"Um." I thought about the mud houses I'd seen. They weren't Sherpa houses. They looked spidery and dark. "Let's keep going. I think I can make it."

We finished our drinks and hoisted our packs. Dropping the bottles off on the way, we walked by the short row of mud houses. Goats and chickens wandered between the small structures.

Grape vines curled around the mud walls. Barefoot children ran out, crying, "Pens, please!"

Suddenly, it hit me. These were Jirels. The houses all looked the same. The children wanted pens. I was too tired to care anymore. I wanted out of the mountains, Jirel or no Jirel.

The next day, we continued on to Jiri. Once again, my stomach cramped, and nausea came in waves. I felt lightheaded and weak. Walking was torturous. The trail seemed steeper than I remembered. Just two weeks ago, hiking felt like a dream. I remembered how excited I was and how fast I walked. Today, Chris kept glancing back. Finally, he stopped.

"I think you need to rehydrate."

"I'm okay," I said.

"No, you're not." He took off his pack and poured some powdered electrolytes into a water bottle. "Drink this."

"Okay." Obediently, I drank the mixture.

I was such a failure. Not only had I not found the Jirels when I first wanted to, but I'd caught some weird bug and now I couldn't hike.

"Keep it. Take sips as you walk." Chris hoisted his pack and turned toward the trail.

I followed. Something else bothered me. Secretly, I'd wanted to return feeling transformed or enlightened, like a vision quest. I thought of the Buddha statue in the monastery at Goli Gompa. I pictured his wide, benevolent smile and the way I felt—as though part of me had come home. But I hadn't found peace. I missed my mom. I had spent a whole afternoon crying in a storage room because I was lonely. I wasn't brave and independent at all.

"Are you going to stay in Jiri and interview more Jirels?" Chris asked.

I sighed. "I'm going back to Kathmandu."

"Want to meet up?"

I studied the back of Chris's knees. His legs were very white. I knew he liked me. He'd been nothing but kind. He made me laugh. He made sure I ate. He took care of everything. No guy had ever been that nice to me. He practically saved my life. Okay, maybe I wouldn't have died in Ringmo, but I felt like I was having a nervous breakdown. Anyway, Chris looked after me. I was totally indebted to him. What did he see in me, anyway? He was much older. I was young and inexperienced. "Maybe. I'll have to see where I'm at with interviews," I lied.

We hiked all morning and into the afternoon. Up, up, up and then down, down, down. I froze on the high passes and sweated in the river bottoms. Gradually, the landscape became more familiar. It looked like the North Cascades with pine trees and great rolling foothills. The air turned warm and balmy. I smelled cooking fires and juniper. On the last pass before Jiri, we stopped for water. I took off my pack and sat on it. Letting the breeze cool my face, I closed my eyes.

Chris sat next to me and pulled out a candy bar. "Want some?"

"No."

"Why don't you eat?"

I opened my eyes. I couldn't read his expression behind his reflective sunglasses. "What do you mean? I'm sick."

"But it's more than that." Chris chewed slowly. "You never eat. Why?"

Suddenly, I felt like I was thirteen again. *Am I in trouble?* "I don't know," I said truthfully. "I just can't sometimes."

"That's not good for you. You know that."

"Yes, I know."

We fell silent. A warm breeze picked up from the valley. In the distance, I could make out the little settlement of houses clinging to the hillside, Jiri. Almost there. I thought about the nuns at the monastery above Junbesi. Maybe I was supposed to come back one day. Maybe I would become a nun. Maybe Buddhism would save me.

An hour later, we stumbled into town. Buses rumbled, and bearded trekkers with bright packs and ski poles walked up and down the main street.

"There's the guesthouse that Kai and I stayed at two weeks ago," I said, pointing.

"Looks good to me."

We found a room on the second floor and dropped our packs near the door.

"Is there a shower?" Chris asked.

"Yes, it's out back." I dug in my pack for a bar of soap and shampoo. "You want to take one first?"

"No, you go ahead."

"Okay." I didn't protest.

The shower was a metal pipe that looped over an old chicken house. I had to balance my feet on two slippery boards that were suspended over a pit of manure. It smelled terrible, but the water ran out hot. It was my first real shower in two weeks. I closed my eyes and held my breath as I let the water stream over my face. Wonderful.

I ran back to the room and found a clean pair of lounge pants and a T-shirt. Someone had left a comb on the windowsill. As I looked out the window, I ran the comb through my hair. I could just make out Jimmy's house, halfway up the mountain. It looked tinier than ever in the setting sun. *Where is Jimmy? Has his brother left for another mountaineering expedition? What about the little girls with dark hair?* Somehow, the thought of them made me sad.

"Wow. That felt good." Chris walked in, dripping water all over the floor. "First shower in weeks, mate." He rummaged through his pack for a clean shirt. "Where's dinner?"

"Downstairs."

"You want to eat now?" He put on his flip-flops.

"Sure." I set down the comb and grabbed my sweater.

We made our way to the dining room. To my surprise, Jimmy greeted me in the doorway. "Hello, sister!" He grinned and grabbed my hand.

"Jimmy." I smiled, laughing. "You're here after all."

"Yes, *didi*. I always here. Work, work, work."

"And you're learning English," I said.

He couldn't keep the smile from his face. "Yes."

A group of trekkers with ponytails and sunburned faces sat at a long table in the middle of the room.

"Hiya, mates," Chris said.

"Hello." They all smiled and nodded.

"Can we join you?"

"Sure." One of the men slid over to make room for us. His blue eyes accented a scruffy beard. "Where are you guys from?"

"New Zealand," Chris said.

"America." I smiled.

"You come from Base Camp?" the bearded guy asked.

"Yep. Bloody hard hike, but worth it," Chris said.

"That's what I hear."

Jimmy arrived to take our order. Everyone seemed to talk at once. They pointed at the menu and ordered large quantities of dal bhat, chapatis, and beer.

"What do you want?" Chris asked me.

"I'll have a chapati." I sipped from my water bottle.

Chris ordered for both of us, then turned to the bearded guy. "You're English."

"Yeah. I'm from Manchester. These blokes are from all over, but mostly we know each other from school."

Chris and the English guy talked about where they lived in London. Letting the conversation flow around me, I thought about Jimmy and the guys working in the kitchen. I waited tables back home in Washington. I knew what it was like to wait on large groups. It was chaotic. Everyone talked at once. They all wanted different things. Sometimes they acted like they owned you. At the far end of the room, an open door led to the kitchen. I saw men bent over a propane cookstove. Someone sat peeling potatoes on the floor. Pots and pans clinked and rattled. When Jimmy arrived with our food, I smiled, hoping he would catch my little message of empathy.

"Let's get another round!" someone said.

"I'll have a beer too," Chris added.

Jimmy set the plates on the table and ran off to fetch more beers. I tore my chapati into little pieces and ate slowly, savoring the chewy texture.

"You want some of mine?" Chris asked.

"No, I'll stick with this. I'll see how my stomach does." I took a sip of water.

Jimmy returned with the beers.

"A toast to Everest Base Camp," the bearded guy said.

"To Base Camp!" Everyone clinked their bottles and cheered.

The evening wore on with more rounds of beer and some kind of clear liquid in shot glasses. The English group grew louder. Chris laughed a lot. I tried a sip of the clear stuff, but it burned my throat. My eyes watered.

"Gross," I said, yawning.

"Yep, I'm done for." Chris pushed his chair back and stood.

We said our goodbyes to the English group and made our way back to the room by candlelight. The village had no electricity after dark. Generators powered a few lights in the kitchens. I leaned out the window. Stars glittered in the black sky. Candles flickered in windows across the street. Bursts of laughter spilled into the night.

Chris set the candle on the wooden apple crate between the two bunks and took off his shirt. "Want a back rub?" he asked.

"Sure." I hesitated.

He patted my sleeping bag and motioned for me to lie down.

I lay still, feeling his hands on my skin. Shadows danced in the candlelight. Dogs barked in the distance. *Is this an invitation for more?* Just a week ago, I had sorted potatoes with the nuns. I wasn't ready for this. Chris leaned down and kissed my neck.

"Don't." I shifted away. *Is this what grownups do? Does everyone hook up with their trekking partners? Is there something wrong with me if I don't?*

"I'm sorry." He stood. Even in the candlelight his face was red.

"No," I said. "It's me. I'm sorry."

"No worries, mate. I'm tuckered out." He flopped onto his sleeping bag.

Silence.

"Good night?" I said.

"Good night." His tone was short.

I lay awake for a long time, listening to the wind and watching the stars rotate in the great black sky.

The next morning, Chris and I boarded a bus headed for Kathmandu. We sat in the back, surrounded by university students on their way to the city. Two of them were learning English, which they eagerly tried out on me. *Do you have a boyfriend? Is Chris your boyfriend? No? Would you like to go out with me?* After each question, they dissolved into laughter. *Do you like pizza? Do you listen to Bob Marley?* The questions went on and on.

Chris glared at the boys. He put his arm around my shoulder. I tried to shrug it off, but he left it, heavy and hot against my skin. I looked out the window. The landscape was turning green and lush. We passed great rushing rivers with sandy beaches and blue swimming holes. Clear water ran over dark rocks, but the swimming holes were all empty. Maybe people didn't swim in Nepal.

When we stopped in the villages, men carrying trays of steaming teacups and packets of chips and peanuts came aboard. "Chai? Chai?" they called. More people crowded on. Some hitched a ride on top with the luggage. As we roared away from the villages, children ran after us, pelting the people on top with rocks and mud.

The narrow dirt road looped around hairpin turns and down steep grades. Every few minutes, the driver stopped for someone to go to the bathroom or to give someone a ride to the next village. The hours crept by. When we approached an oncoming bus, we had to stop. Men up front tapped on the window, and the driver honked his horn as the two buses inched by each other. Stuck in the back, I could hardly breathe. There was no air.

"Bloody hell," said Chris. "This is ridiculous."

We arrived at the bus station in Kathmandu just after eight at night. Chris was irate because he had promised to meet up with some trekking buddies that night. "I'm late."

We staggered off the bus, lugging our backpacks. "Do you want to meet in Thamel this week?" Chris asked.

"Sure." We stood on the side of the road, waiting for a cab. I could smell diesel fuel and sewage. The sun had set, leaving the city cast in shadows. A warm breeze scattered papers and plastic bottles down the street.

"There's a cab." Chris stepped up to the curb with my backpack. "What's your address?"

"132 Jawalekhel, near the temple."

The cab driver poked his head out of the window. Chris gave him my address and put my pack in the trunk. He turned to face me. "I'll see you Wednesday. Helena's Bakery, three-o-clock."

"Wednesday." I nodded. I felt a lump in my throat. "Chris . . ." I touched his hand. "Thank you . . . you know, for everything."

He grinned and kissed me on the lips. Then he turned away and tapped the roof of the taxi. I couldn't see his face.

As we pulled away from the curb, I looked back. Chris stood pale and alone, among hundreds of Nepalis, waiting for a different cab.

CHAPTER FOURTEEN

⊲❑◉❑◉❑◉◉◉❑◉◉❑◉❑❑◉⊳

I WIPED A CLEAN circle on the grimy bus window and peered out. The sky was just beginning to lighten. Between the shadows, banana, mango, and palm trees appeared. Chickens pecked at the ground. Mud houses lined the road where men squatted near their fires. Inside the bus, the air felt heavy and hot. I pressed my face against the cracked window, breathing in the earthy aroma of jungle, smoke, and frying chapatis.

Traveling with Mary, a Nepali missionary woman who didn't speak a word of English, was driving me crazy. I was on my way to Dharan, a city on the southern border of Nepal and India. I was trying to find the Lepcha people, but after leaving Kathmandu and spending all night on the bus, I just wanted to go home. Hindi pop music blared from the crackling speakers, and the little elephant god, Ganesh, danced on the dashboard.

An odd sort of apathy had plagued me for the past few days. I was supposed to meet Chris at the bakery in Kathmandu, but I was late coming back from an appointment with a local college professor. When I arrived at the bakery, Chris had already left. I ordered a latte and watched tourists as they laughed and talked. A couple next to me were discussing esoteric books on the meaning of life. I felt lonely and depressed. Studying a bulletin board, I noticed a flyer that read, "Krishnamurti Consciousness Meeting." It was at the bookstore across the street. I looked at the date, today. Actually, right now.

"Is this the Krishna meeting?" I asked the Nepali guy behind the counter. He pointed to a staircase at the back of the store.

On the second floor, in a spacious room with big windows, a bunch of Western tourists sat on the floor. A few Nepalis stood near the back. Several men were smoking joints, and a girl with flowing white pants and a halter top sat quietly with her eyes closed. She was humming. Many of the attendees had piercings, dreadlocks, and lots of tattoos.

A short, balding man with glasses stood up front. His nametag read, "Dr. Krishna." Someone handed me a brochure. The lecture was entitled, "Why Man Has Not Changed." Dr. Krishna began by explaining that man had not changed since Neolithic times. Once, we killed each other with spears. Now, we dropped atomic bombs. Our basic consciousness had remained the same.

"How can this be?" he asked. "We have lived through great leaders such as Christ, the Buddha, and Gandhi. But," he said as he adjusted his scarf around his neck, "we have not changed. Why? Our differences are only an illusion." His calm voice droned on and on.

Suddenly, I heard chanting. I glanced out the window. A crowd had gathered in the street, and a man riding in the back of a truck held a megaphone to his lips. He shouted something in Nepali over and over. The crowded chanted back. *What are they yelling? Is it a political movement?* Inside, everyone seemed to ignore the growing disturbance.

Dr. Krishna went on with his lecture. "We need to change our inner selves."

The audience nodded. A few murmured in agreement. A hand shot up.

Dr. Krishna pushed his glasses up on his nose. "Yes?"

"What can we do about all the bad energies in the world?" The girl had a pale face with freckles. She wore a monk's robe and prayer beads.

Dr. Krishna nodded and sighed. "That is a very good question. There will always be bad energy in the world. When we think a negative thought or have a negative feeling, it goes into the universe. It affects everything. The only way is to change your response to the world."

A young Nepali man in a white shirt and tie stood near the back of the room. Shifting his weight, he looked agitated. He spoke with impeccable English. "Teacher, what does this have to do with the poor whose stomachs are empty? Shall we tell them it is just an illusion?" He leaned forward. His eyes glared at the speaker. The air in the room felt tense.

Dr. Krishna held out his hand. "Everything is an illusion," he intoned. "We must all settle the storms within ourselves. This is the only way to true freedom."

I glanced at the Nepali man. His lips tightened. He stood with his arms folded over his chest. After several minutes, he left the room. I wanted to leave too. I had hoped for an enlightening talk, but something didn't match up between the people shouting outside and the hippie tourists inside. I didn't know what the chanting was all about, but the Nepali man brought up a good point. How could I tell the beggar across the street that there was no difference between us? I had privileges that he would never have. I wanted to believe in something, but this was not it.

Later that week, I attended a wedding. Apparently, the Christian community in Nepal was so small that the men sent away for brides. The bride's name was Lottie. She was from Mexico. Before the wedding, she'd cut my hair and we'd get together for tea. Her fiancé, Keshor, was from Nepal. His brother had arranged the marriage.

When I arrived at the house, Lottie was trying on her wedding dress. With her dark eyes and long black hair, the white dress was striking against her skin. She looked beautiful and absolutely terrified.

"Hello." I knocked lightly against the doorframe.

"Ah, Julie." Lottie looked up and tears welled in her eyes. "It doesn't fit."

"It looks beautiful."

"It's too tight." She smoothed her hand over the bodice.

"No, no. It's perfect." I reached down and arranged the long train.

She gave a tiny smile. "Not too tight?"

"Not at all." I hugged her shoulders. "You're going to be fine."

She took a deep, shaky breath and let it out slowly. "I'm nervous."

"You're going to be fine," I repeated.

"I'm nervous about tonight." She looked at me. "I don't really know him."

"He seems like a very nice man."

"Yes, but he's so much older."

I didn't know what to say. I was out of my league on this one.

Louisa, my roommate, walked in. "Everyone's ready. We'll walk to the church now."

Lottie gripped my hand. I gave hers a squeeze. "Good luck."

The ceremony took place in the church courtyard. Because Christianity is illegal in Nepal, the church was an inauspicious looking building with a small yard. I watched the proceedings from the back of the crowd. Keshor stood straight and stiff. He looked uncomfortable in his black suit and tie. Sweat glistened on his temples. It was hot. Tears ran down Lottie's cheeks as she said her vows first in Spanish. She repeated the words slowly in Nepali. She didn't speak the language yet. Finally, she said the vows in English. The thirty or so in attendance clapped and threw rice. It was over.

I couldn't imagine moving to another country to marry someone I'd never met. I knew arranged marriage was common in Nepal, but I had never been to one. I felt sad for the couple. They both looked scared.

I walked home after the ceremony. Louisa and Manek, the missionary couple, stayed behind for dinner, but I didn't feel like socializing. The setting sun cast a golden light over the brick buildings. A slight wind tugged at my skirt. I recognized the Gurkha soldier near the military base. He smiled as I passed. The old man at the grocer's stand nodded. People were beginning to recognize me. What would it be like to live here? Crossing the street, I noticed a young man begging on the side of the road. I couldn't help but stare. His left cheek was all puffed up and sloughing off. His nose was twisted sidewise, disappearing into the flesh. He had no fingers or toes. He was a leper. He met my eyes, and I felt my face flush. *How does he get up in the morning? How does he keep going?* Sometimes the poverty in Kathmandu overwhelmed me. I didn't know how to respond.

When I got home, the house felt big and empty. Next door, children were setting off fireworks. Tonight, they would light candles in the windowsills to remind Lakshmi, as she circled the world at midnight, to bless them. I sat in the dark listening to the children sing and the wind moving over the rooftops.

Now, peering out the bus window, I felt depressed and exhausted. *Will Keshor and Lottie be happy in their new marriage? Has Chris left for New Zealand, or is he still in Kathmandu? Will he forget about me?* And something about the Krishnamurti meeting both intrigued and repelled me. *Who is actually bettering the world? The tourists with their nose rings and deep consciousness or the missionaries with their Bibles and social programs?*

The bus groaned to a stop. I grabbed my pack and followed Mary and her friend. Pink clouds stretched across the sky. Tropical birds sang in jacaranda trees. Purple flowers hung from the spreading branches. The streets were crowded with people selling cardamoms, cinnamon, cloves, oranges, bananas, and nuts. Meat vendors waved newspapers to keep the flies off. A strange fish with glassy eyes caught my attention. It smelled rancid. We passed people selling mangos, pomegranates, coconuts, and pineapples. Someone was roasting peanuts over a little fire. As I trailed behind Mary and her friend, a man grabbed my arm. Another touched my hair. They laughed. Their dark faces were filled with curiosity and a faint touch of hostility. They spoke Hindi instead of Nepali. I yanked my arm away and shook my head. Maybe I should have worn the headscarf Lottie gave me. She said I'd need it here.

We trudged through the city until we came to a yellow house with a dove painted above the entrance. Through the wrought-iron gate, I saw green grass and hibiscus bushes. Rhododendrons grew around the border, and orange trees dangled green fruit. A calm, slender man with graying hair and a clerical collar met us in the courtyard.

He bowed low. "Hello." He held out his hand. "I am Pastor B.B. Rai."

"Hello." I smiled.

Mary and her friend spoke to him in Nepali.

B.B. Rai turned to me. "You will have a wash and rest for a bit." He pointed to the house. "Later, my son will take you to the missionary base." We followed him to an upstairs room with yellow walls and a smooth tiled floor. The room was empty except for a pile of grass mats in the corner and a sink at one end. B.B. Rai spread out three mats and patted one. "You can rest here." Bowing low, he left the room. Mary and her friend took off their headscarves and washed their faces. They lay down and slept almost immediately.

I was too hot to sleep. I lay on the mat and stared at the ceiling fan above my head. *What am I doing here with these Christian missionaries?* They seemed kind. I wished I was a nice missionary girl. Guilty, I glanced at my copies of *The Snow Leopard* by Peter Matthiessen and *Think on These Things* by Jiddu Krishnamurti. Thankfully, Mary and her friend didn't speak English. No one would know that I was reading a Buddhist memoir or the teachings of a Hindu guru. I closed my eyes and tried to sleep, but Mary and her friend were snoring. Quietly, I reached for the book by Krishnamurti. I was on chapter eleven, "Conformity and Revolt." Flipping the page, I read:

> *From the moment you are born and begin to receive impressions, your father and mother are constantly telling you what to do and what not to do, what to believe and what not to believe; you are told that there is God or there is no God.*

That was ironic. He went on to say that every thought we have is a product of our culture and society. Although we think we are free, we are prisoners inside our minds. He recommended going to a solitary place and watching your thoughts come and go.

> *Your mind is humanity, and when you perceive this, you will have immense compassion. Out of this understanding comes great love, and then you will know when you see lovely things, what beauty is.*

I wanted immense compassion and understanding. As an apprentice of anthropology, I understood that our culture shapes the way we see the world. Could I learn to see through a different cultural lens than the one I grew up with? Gazing at the ceiling, I watched the fan spin round and round. I tried to observe my thoughts. I thought of the orange tree in the garden and how much I'd rather be outside. A cup of coffee would be nice and maybe a Danish. No, a Danish would be indulgent, too much fat. Fat was bad. I was still trying to stay thin after my trek. I imagined myself home at Christmastime, three sizes smaller.

"Where have you been?" my friends would ask.

"Nepal," I'd say casually.

"Wow," they'd say.

Maybe I'd run into the guy I liked. Would he have a girlfriend by now? Would she be skinnier than me? My thoughts went on and on. I had forgotten to watch them. Within seconds, I was lost in the grand narrative inside my head. I slept.

CHAPTER FIFTEEN

◁❑◉❑◉❑◉◉◉◉❑◉❑◉◉❑❑▷

WHEN I WOKE UP, Mary and her friend were gone. I walked to the window. The garden was empty. *Where is everyone?* I looked around. Nothing to eat. At least I had my water bottle. The room felt hot and stuffy. *It must be about lunchtime.* I returned to the mat and tried to meditate. I closed my eyes and breathed. I watched a thought arise, then another and another. Within seconds, my thoughts were swirling inside my head like snow in wintertime. This was ridiculous. I didn't feel at peace. I felt like I was going crazy. I walked back to the window. If only I could be in that garden. *Could I go down there? Maybe I should wait for someone to come to me.* All afternoon, I stared down at the orange tree. No one came, and I was too scared to leave.

After what seemed like forever, I heard a soft tap at the door. It was B.B. Rai.

"Hello." I tried to look cheerful.

"Ah, you must be rested. Are you ready to go?"

"Yes."

I followed him into the garden. Someone was playing Christian music on a guitar.

"Tell me about your studies." B.B. Rai patted my shoulder and motioned for me to sit.

"I'm an anthropology major." *Does he know what that is?*

"Ah yes, anthropology. We need anthropologists here." B.B. Rai took off his glasses and polished them on his sleeve. "The Lepcha are a little-known people. Their numbers are very, very small. We are pleased that you have come."

"Thank you." I was embarrassed. I wasn't really an anthropologist; not yet. I was only in my second year of college. I wanted to ask more about the Lepcha, but a young man strolled into the garden.

"Ah." B.B. Rai rose. "This is my son, Rasu."

Rasu smiled and shook my hand. He had light-brown hair and a calm demeanor. Rasu and his father could have been twins.

"Hello. My name is Julie."

"She is from America." B.B. Rai turned to Rasu. "She is an anthropologist."

"Very nice." Rasu nodded.

The late evening sun streamed into the garden. *Shouldn't we be going?* I was beginning to understand that Nepalis operate on a different schedule than Westerners. They take their time. No one hurries for anything.

B.B. Rai said something to Rasu in Nepali. The two conversed. I shifted my feet. I hadn't eaten today, and now my stomach clenched with hunger.

At last, Rasu motioned to me. "Come."

I followed him into the street, where a small motorbike leaned on its kickstand. Rasu hopped on and patted the seat behind him. I swung my leg over and hesitated. "It's okay." Rasu patted his stomach. I felt awkward hugging a man I'd just met, but I liked the idea of a motorbike ride through the city.

B.B. Rai followed us to the street. He handed me a card. "Here is my telephone number," he said. "If you need anything, call me."

"Thank you. I will." I waved.

Rasu gunned the engine, and we rumbled down the street.

Dharan reminded me of India. Stucco houses lined the dirt roads in various shades of lime green, baby blue, magenta, and pink. Men with scarves around their heads and wearing loose-fitting skirts sold fried chapatis and boiled eggs over cookstoves. Women in saris carried jerry cans of water on their heads, and dogs wandered through the streets. We careened down alley after alley, swerving around potholes and big white cows. Gone were the brick buildings and ornate wooden doorways of Kathmandu. Instead, wrought-iron bars and gates surrounded every house. Hindi music blared from radios. The sky looked soft, warmer than Kathmandu. The stars, as they appeared, looked yellower and far away. Even in the dark, I could sense the great Indian subcontinent stretching away to the south.

The missionary base was a sprawling single-level compound near the edge of the city. Rasu killed the engine. I slipped off the bike and followed him to the house. The front door stood open. We heard people talking inside.

"*Namaste,*" Rasu called, knocking lightly on the doorframe. A man wearing a faded blue T-shirt and reading glasses appeared. He had dark eyebrows and straight black hair. He'd been eating something. Now, he cleared his throat and wiped his mouth. "Ah." He clasped my hand. "You must be Julie. We've been waiting for you all day. Come."

I'd been waiting all day too. Rasu turned to leave. "Good luck, Julie."

"Thank you." I waved and followed the man with glasses.

"I am Obed," he said over his shoulder.

Obed led me down a bright-blue hallway. The house reminded me of the places I'd stayed in India, probably built for a polygamous family. Several bedrooms lay off a central kitchen that opened onto a concrete patio surrounded by walls and iron gates. As we passed the kitchen, I saw a young girl stirring something over a large black pot. I sniffed. Rice. I hoped they would offer me some. Obed motioned toward a room with brown tiles across from the kitchen. I looked around. There was no furniture, just grass mats like I'd seen at B.B. Rai's house.

"Please sit." Obed pulled out two mats. Outside, the night hummed with crickets. He leaned forward. "What brings you to Dharan, Julie?"

Didn't he know? Louisa said she'd talked to someone on the telephone before my arrival. I wasn't sure where to start.

"I am an anthropology student," I said. I explained that I wanted to find the Lepcha people of eastern Nepal. I had read about them in my ethnography books. No one knew much about them. They lived somewhere on the border between Nepal and Sikkim.

"Do you have a map?" Obed asked.

"Yes." I pulled out the map of eastern Nepal that I had purchased in Kathmandu.

Obed peered through his glasses. "No," he muttered. "Not good enough. Kirja!" He shouted. A slim young man appeared in the doorway. Rubbing his hand across his face, Obed said something in Nepali. The young man left, returning minutes later with a large roll of paper. Obed spread the map on the floor.

"Kirja is from Ilam," Obed explained. "He should know where the Lepcha live." Only recently had the Lepcha become farmers. Traditionally, an indigenous hunter-gatherer group, they lived in scattered hamlets. They had no consolidated villages. English missionaries brought them Christianity and farming. Now, they raised tea and cardamom in the eastern foothills.

"Very hard to find," Kirja said. "I know some, but is very far." He tapped the map with his finger. "Cold in Lepcha-land. Rugged too."

I was embarrassed. How rude for me to show up alone and unchaperoned. Now, I was their responsibility. Running his hands through his hair, Obed sighed. "I think we will wait and see."

Wait and see about what? Should I go back to Kathmandu? Is there anyone who knows where the Lepcha live?

A young girl came to the door and said something to Obed.

"It is time to eat." He motioned outside. About twelve students sat in a large circle on the ground. They all looked about my age. I hesitated. Where to sit? The students smiled and ducked their heads shyly. One girl scooted over and patted the ground. I sat next to her.

The little girl gave everyone a plate, and Obed walked around serving rice and lentils. We ate without spoons or forks. The students watched as I lumped the rice together with my fingers and tried to get it into my mouth without spilling it. A few of them giggled and looked away. I glanced around at the group. Two young men sat together. They didn't speak Nepali or Hindi. The girls had shiny black hair and large nose rings. Obed took a seat across from me. I got the feeling he was not particularly pleased that I had come, but he was too polite to say so.

"Is everyone here Nepali?" I asked Obed.

"No. Those two." He gestured toward the young men sitting together. "One is from Korea and the other from Japan. The girls are from India. And . . ." He glanced around the group. "Only Kirja is from Nepal."

"Students from Korea and Japan?" I was surprised.

Obed shrugged. "It is YWAM, a big organization. You are not with YWAM?"

"No." I wiped my mouth. "I am only staying with Manek and Louisa in Kathmandu. But I am familiar with it." I hoped he wouldn't ask more.

Just as we finished eating, two men with backpacks arrived. "Ah, this is Temjin and Omar. They have returned from Kathmandu. They are leaders." He rose to his feet. "Excuse me, I must speak with them." The students seemed pleased to see the men. They jumped up, laughing and speaking at once. Temjin, a wiry man in his mid-thirties, clapped the boys on the back and said something that made them laugh. Omar had smooth skin and a calm demeanor. He helped himself to a plate of food and joined Temjin and Obed in the room with the brown tiled floor. They closed the door.

I followed the students to the kitchen. We rinsed our plates in a big tub filled with water. There was no soap. We waved them dry and stacked them on the shelf. I wasn't sure what to do next. Behind the closed door, I heard the men's voices talking animatedly. Every so often I recognized a "Julie or "American." They were talking about me. I wandered outside and sat on the patio.

At last, Obed appeared, looking relieved. "We have decided that you will stay here for a few days. There is a schoolteacher who lives near Ninda. She is going up to Lepcha-land next week. You will go with her."

"Thank you," I said. "I hope I'm not intruding . . ."

"No, no, it is fine. Tomorrow is a national holiday. No buses. No trains." He paused. "Would you like to see some dancing?"

"Sure." What kind of dancing was he talking about? We walked across the dark patio and through a gate into the neighbor's backyard.

"They are Hindu," Obed whispered. "The children have been practicing for Tihar, the festival of lights." He explained that during Tihar, girls go door to door dancing for money. "It is a big holiday, five days long," he said. Each day is devoted to a particular animal or theme. One day, people honor the dog. Another day, the cow. They decorate the animals with marigolds and paint and give offerings of milk and treats. The children waved to us, happy to have an audience as they practiced for Tihar. They wore bright saris and little pointed shoes. They moved quickly, their fingers curved in *mudras*, or symbols. Their heads bobbed sideways.

"I have never seen this dance," Obed said.

"Really?"

"No, I am from Nagaland."

"Nagaland?" This intrigued me. It sounded like a fairy tale. I almost laughed.

"Northern India, across the border."

"You're not Nepali?" I asked.

"No, no. I am Naga. I do not speak Nepali or Hindi, but I am learning." He rubbed his forehead. "Language is very difficult for me."

"But you speak English," I said.

"Yes, from boarding school."

We watched the children silently. I wanted to ask him more about Nagaland and boarding school, but his face looked stern.

How old is he? I couldn't tell. Now that he'd said it, I realized he didn't look Nepali at all. Most Nepali men didn't have facial hair. He obviously shaved.

At last, Obed said, "I think you are tired now, yes?"

"Yes." But I wasn't.

We went back to the compound. Obed showed me to the girls' room and gave me a half-inch foam sleeping mat. "Good night," he said.

"Good night."

I turned to face the girls. They stared as if waiting for me to do something miraculous. Their dark eyes sparkled. *What am I supposed do?* I glanced around the room, which was bare except for the sleeping mats. *Where is their stuff? Don't they have clothes or luggage?* This was their room, yet there were no dressers, no bags, no closet. The girls had only their flip-flops, which they placed neatly next to the door, and a Bible for evening prayers. I smiled. "Hello."

They grinned and said "Hello" back. They said it carefully, pronouncing each syllable. One girl made room for my mat next to hers. I set my pack down and pulled out my sweater. One by one, the girls settled onto their mats. A few had silver ankle bracelets that jingled as they moved. Their toenails were painted bright pink. Before sleeping, each girl knelt on her mat, folded her hands tightly, and prayed out loud for several minutes. Their rapid Hindi sounded like a song rising and falling. When they were done praying, they lay down and closed their eyes.

How could I sleep without a pillow or blanket? The night air was hot, and I wasn't used to sleeping on a bare floor. I wadded up my sweater and put it under my head. One of the girls turned off the light. In a few minutes, their breathing grew slow and even. I lay awake for a long time. Mosquitoes whined around my ears. I should have purchased malaria pills before I left Kathmandu.

In the morning, I felt tired and sluggish. Once again, I found myself at the mercy of my hosts with nothing to do. I spent the next two days hanging around the compound, shopping with the girls or waiting for Obed's random appearances. Obed spent much of his time elsewhere. I didn't know what he did all day. When he arrived, he always looked the same: calm, patient, and serious. When he saw me, I noticed that his face was often flush.

One night, after dinner, I sat outside with the students. The Korean guy played his guitar while someone else sang. Inside, I could see Obed wandering around the kitchen. *Is he looking for me?* He glanced outside before walking over.

I smiled. "Hello."

"How is Julie this evening?" He sat next to me in the cool grass.

"Fine." I waited for him to say something, but he didn't. Finally, I said, "Tell me about Nagaland."

He smiled. Leaning back on his elbows, he talked about the jungles and hills of Nagaland. "It was beautiful. Very green. Lots of rain. Flowers. There were warriors in Nagaland." He looked at me. "My grandfather was a warrior. He was a headhunter. You know, a cannibal."

"Really?"

Obed shook his head. "Yes, but then Christianity came, and everyone changed very quickly. That was a long time ago."

It didn't seem like that long ago to me. It sounded fascinating. Cannibals? Headhunters? His grandfather? I shivered happily.

"Everything is different now. Men and women are treated equally. There is no more headhunting. Everyone goes to school and learns English as well as Naga." He was quiet for a minute. "The main problem we have is that it's difficult to find a Christian wife."

"Why?" I asked.

"The Hindu women tend to be . . . more conservative, you know?"

I shook my head. "How do you mean?"

"They are less exposed to modern ways and new ideas. The Christian community is quite small. There are only a few." He scratched his head and fell silent.

Is that why he's here with YWAM? To find a Christian wife?

"How old are you?" I asked, curious.

His face flushed. "I am thirty-one."

"Do you have a girlfriend?" I knew I was prying, but I wanted to know.

Obed shook his head. "No. I don't have time. I work too hard."

It didn't seem like anyone worked too hard to me, but I had no idea what it took to run a mission's organization in Dharan. Obed intrigued me. For some reason, I liked him better than Chris. He was older, but he had an innocence that made me feel safe.

When I left on the morning bus, two days later, Obed was nowhere to be found. Would I ever see him again? I hoped so.

CHAPTER SIXTEEN

THE BUS TO NINDA wound across the Terai, stopping to pick up passengers. Women, children, goats, and chickens crowded on. Outside, the flat landscape stretched out as far as I could see. Elephant grass waved in the breeze. Shimmering heat reflected against the red-dirt road. The Terai was a rich grassland that stretched from the foothills of the Himalayas to northern India. Rare animals like the sloth bear, the Indian rhinoceros, and the Bengal tiger lived in the protected jungles and savannas. Peering out the window, I saw fields of yellow mustard and corn.

I was traveling with Temjin, one of the missionary leaders. Like Obed, he was from Nagaland. Maybe they knew each other from school. Or maybe they were related. Temjin had a strange, almost elfin face. He laughed and joked constantly. Today, he bobbed his head and sang, "Buffalo soldier . . . stolen from Africa. Brought to America . . ."

I gazed out the window, trying not to let the song get stuck in my head. The hours passed. Finally, I said, "Please, stop. Your singing is driving me crazy."

"You don't like Bob Marley?"

"Sometimes."

"How about this? 'Rise up this morning . . . smiled with the rising sun.' " He grinned, snapping his fingers in the air.

I laughed and covered my ears. "No! I'll never get it out of my head."

"Why don't you like Bob Marley? I thought all Americans like Bob."

"I don't know. Some people do. Why do Nepalis love Bob Marley?"

"Because it's groovy, you know, snappy. And also," he said, then paused, thinking about it, "we can relate."

Over the last few months and all over the countryside, I had seen the Communist swastika and sickle painted on walls and abandoned buildings. Nepal had been a democratic republic for only five years. The Communist party was agitating for a seat in the government. A university professor in Kathmandu said that Communism might be best for Nepal. Something had to address the crushing poverty and the huge number of peasants. Even I could sense the national mood. It felt as if the whole country was holding its breath, waiting for something to happen. Maybe Bob Marley's freedom songs reflected this mood.

After several hours, we arrived at a village tucked inside a thick, dark jungle. Houses made from red clay with thatched roofs nestled between tall deciduous trees. Smoke drifted out of the windows.

"Magar!" Temjin shouted above the shrieking brakes. The bus came to a sudden stop in a cloud of dust.

"What?" I shouted back.

"Magar village."

"Oh," I said. The Magars were closely related to the Jirels from Solu Khumbu. I recognized the houses—just like Jimmy's back in Jiri. Here, I would meet the schoolteacher who was going to Lepcha-land, another day's travel to the north.

We stumbled off the bus. I took a deep breath. The air

smelled of cooking fires and wet earth. Puddles of water stood in the road. I followed Temjin down a narrow dirt track with tall, drooping trees and thick ropelike vines. Strange birds sang from the trees' canopy. Mosquitos swarmed at my arms. We stopped at one of the houses. Chickens scratched and pecked in the dirt. A goat, tethered to an old tire, bleated at us.

"Namaste!" Temjin hollered and knocked at the door. The house sat still and empty. He knocked again. We waited. At last, a young girl wandered up from somewhere behind the house. She frowned. Temjin said something in Hindi. She shook her head.

"Ke garne," Temjin muttered under his breath.

"What's that?" I asked.

"Ke garne. It means, 'what to do' when things don't work out. Shanti's not here."

The girl led us inside. A cooking fire smoldered in a clay oven. A couple of guinea hens squawked and fluffed their feathers before returning to their perch in the corner. The girl pointed to a bamboo ladder tied together with vines that disappeared through a hole in the low ceiling. Carefully, we climbed the ladder and found ourselves on the second floor. It swayed as we walked. Glancing up, I saw that the roof was made from bamboo thatch. The floor, covered with grass mats, must be the same. Smoke seeped up through the thatch. I coughed. Plastic sheets stapled between the bamboo frames formed the interior. Deep cracks ran up and down the mud walls. The whole house shook under our weight. I sat, hardly daring to breathe. Would it hold our weight? Temjin, however, strode across the floor and flopped down on his back.

"What do we do now?" I asked.

"Wait." He yawned and closed his eyes.

"I'm okay to be here alone," I said. "You don't have to wait with me."

"I'll stay for a while."

We sat in silence. Outside, children squealed and laughed in the distance. Cows mooed. Someone shuffled by, humming a tune. I could hear their bare feet in the dirt. People with bare feet walked differently than people with shoes. Shoeless people had to watch where they stepped.

After a couple of hours, the front door rattled. Someone burst into the room downstairs. We heard a loud female voice. Waking from our stupor, Temjin and I glanced at each other.

"Shanti." Temjin rolled his eyes.

Shanti poked her head up through the hole in the floor. "Tea! You must come down for tea," she said excitedly. "Come, come!" She had a round face and dark hair. She looked to be about my age. Shanti beamed at us.

Temjin grabbed his pack.

"Are you leaving?" I asked.

"No, you must stay." Shanti crossed the floor and grabbed Temjin's hand, firing off another stream of Nepali.

Temjin shook his head and made for the ladder. "Goodbye, Julie. Safe travels. We will see you on your way back." He was gone.

Shanti turned to me and grasped my hands. "I am so glad you have come!" She talked as if she had known me forever. "We have much catching up to do."

Shanti spoke English—a lot of it. I was soon overwhelmed by her nonstop chatter. I learned that she lived with her father, who was away in Lepcha-land. We would join him tomorrow. She told me about her newly married sister, Rebecca, and her father's work as a pastor in this village. Shanti was a schoolteacher.

"Ah, Julie." She looked at me and shook her head. "Life in a village is very boring. You must have an exciting life." She stoked the fire as she talked. She hoped to have children someday, but so far, she had no husband. "I don't really want one now." She handed me tea in a small, clear shot glass. "Do you want a husband now? I bet you don't either." She shook her head. "Americans are very independent. I know."

I tried to think of something to say, but I couldn't get a word in edgewise.

Shanti sipped her tea quickly. "I will show you the village. Come." She grabbed my arm, and we headed outside.

Arm in arm, we walked through the village. Women with baskets on their heads stopped to stare at me. Children ran up and patted my skin and pulled on my dress. Shanti waved at the women and shooed away the children. She kept up a constant stream of conversation, telling me about each person in detail; who they were, what they'd done, if they were liked or not, who they were married to, and on and on. Dirt roads connected the scattered red-clay houses. White cows with long horns wandered along the roads, nibbling at the grass. Men worked in the fields, cutting grain with long handheld scythes.

"Why don't people have chimneys?" I asked. It had been bothering me for weeks.

"What is chimney?" Shanti scratched her head.

"Something for the smoke? You know, a tube in the house." I made a circle with my hands.

"Ah . . ." Shanti thought about it. "Is too expensive for most. People build their house and make mud all the way to the top." She held her hand high above her head. "Too much work."

Just about everyone I met coughed. I recognized the sound from my time with Jimmy. Lung infections must be common here.

Shanti showed me the school where she taught. Built by the government, it was an industrial-looking building with yellow brick walls surrounded by a large, empty field. The Nepalese flag fluttered proudly from the roof.

By the time we got back to Shanti's house, my head felt like it might explode. I couldn't keep up with her nonstop chatter. I sat on a stool in front of the fire while she heated water for drinking and stirred something in a black pot.

"You must be very hungry," she said. "This will make you full."

Shanti handed me a bowl of broth swimming with chunks of meat. Upon closer inspection, I saw that the chunks were actually pig fat, cut from a pig's rump with the skin and hair still attached. I stared at the bowl. I couldn't eat it.

"Thank you," I said. "This looks great." I took a sip of broth. It tasted like water, no salt or flavoring. Just the boiled chunks.

Shanti watched me closely. She had saved the meat and bones for herself and given me the fat. Was this intentional? Was she being stingy, or did she think I would rather have this?

"You know, I'm very full," I said, gumming down a bite. The hairs stuck in my mouth. I gagged.

"Oh no, you must eat. Eat!" Shanti commanded.

"Thank you, but this is too much." I handed her the bowl.

Shanti paused, then shrugged and quickly consumed both bowls. She licked her fingers happily and belched. Maybe she had given me the prized pieces. Maybe fat was a luxury here. Belching was a sign of pleasure. She obviously enjoyed the food.

We washed the dishes in a basin on the floor. Then Shanti showed me to the toilet. It was a tiny outhouse made of bamboo and leaves with a hole in the ground. Walking back to the house, I gasped. Stars twinkled brightly in the black sky. There was no moon and no lights in the village. No electricity.

Inside, I told Shanti I was tired. "Where shall I sleep?"

Shanti pointed upstairs. We climbed up the ladder and found a sheet for me to sleep under. She patted one of the grass mats. "This is your mat," she said.

"Thank you." I took a deep breath. I thought sleeping in Dharan was rough. I lay on the mat and tucked my sweater under my head. I pulled up the thin sheet.

Shanti went back downstairs. I could hear her moving around and stoking the fire.

The night air pressed around me, sticky and hot. No breeze. Children cried in the distance. Something shuffled outside. I heard a high-pitched squeal. Then, silence. Pigs. They must hunt wild pigs here. That was what we'd had for dinner.

CHAPTER SEVENTEEN

◁❑◉❑◉❑◉◉◉◉◉❑◉❑◉●❑◉▷

SHANTI SHOOK ME AWAKE. "Wake up, Julie. We must leave."

I glanced out the window. Still dark outside. I was sick of these early-morning bus rides. Yawning, I gathered my things and joined Shanti downstairs.

The time did nothing to curb Shanti's chatter. As I sipped my tea, she continued with wherever she had left off from last night. She talked about the men in the village who didn't appreciate educated women. It wasn't that I didn't care about her anecdotes. I knew having a willing informant was key to ethnographic fieldwork. Yet her obvious faith and my lack of it lay between us like the Grand Canyon. She took it for granted that I was a Christian. I felt like an imposter. Questioning my faith over the past few years filled me with dread. I didn't care so much that I didn't believe anymore. I cared that I didn't have the courage to admit it to others. Worse still, I realized as Shanti talked that her father was hosting a revival meeting in Lepcha-land. I couldn't believe my luck. I was heading into the very thing I had come to abhor.

"Come, Julie. We must go now," she said.

I followed Shanti into the gray, still morning. Roosters crowed. Men, sleeping in their huts, coughed and spat. Already, the air felt warm and sticky. At the bus station, we met a young woman wearing a blue dress and a white sweater. With a heart-shaped face and large brown eyes, she was beautiful.

"This is my sister, Rebecca," Shanti said.

Rebecca smiled and shook my hand. She spoke softly in Nepali. I gathered she didn't speak English. I had no idea what she had said to me.

"Hello," I said.

We stood around drinking chai out of little glasses and waiting for the bus. At last, we heard a diesel engine. The bus ground to a stop before us. Hindi music blared from the speakers, and men hanging from the sides hopped off.

The bus took us deep into the eastern foothills. It followed the border between Sikkim and Nepal before heading north into the mountains. The landscape turned greener and steeper. The roads began to twist and turn. Mustard and corn gave way to cardamoms and tea plantations.

"We must hike three hours tonight to Ninda! You will be very tired," Shanti said, smiling.

Every so often, the bus stopped to drop people off, but no one got on. I daydreamed as I sat next to Shanti, watching the landscape float by. We careened around a sharp corner, and everyone murmured excitedly. I sat up and looked out the window, but I couldn't see anything wrong. I stared into the large rearview mirror. The bus driver wore dark sunglasses that nearly covered his entire face. A cigarette dangled from his lips. He revved the engine. A few of the men sitting near the front jumped off. Craning my neck, I tried to see what was happening. I gasped. The river ahead didn't have a bridge!

I wanted to leap from the bus, but Shanti had me pinned against the window. I couldn't move. The bus rocked back and forth as the driver gunned the engine. The bus lurched forward.

"Good grief, Shanti. Is he going to drive us through the river?"

Shanti sat up and tried to see down the aisle.

The tires slipped and slid over the steep embankment and into the rushing water. I held my breath and closed my eyes. For a moment, I could feel the wheels as they left the ground. We were floating. It seemed like it was forever until the tires dug deeply into the opposite bank. Everyone on board cheered loudly. I breathed in a huge sigh of relief.

The bus continued up the steep trail into the dark-green foothills. The landscape reminded me of a fairy tale with enormous trees that spread out for miles. Sunlit glades were scattered across the landscape. At last, the road petered into a trail and the bus could go no farther. Everyone clambered out.

"Now, we must walk," Shanti said. Gripping my arm, she led me up the trail. Her tiny steps did not match my wide strides. We stumbled. I tried to wrench away, but her fingers tightened around my arm. I felt like a rare animal she had caught and wanted to keep. Realizing that she was not about to let go, I ignored her strong hold.

Shanti pointed out various tea fields and oak trees. I recognized bird of paradise flowers, hibiscus, and plumeria, but many of the plants and trees were foreign to me.

"The Lepchas live there." Shanti pointed across the forested ridgeline. "They are very, very shy. No one speaks Lepcha so . . . how do you say, they are secretive?"

"They keep to themselves?" I prompted.

"Yes! They don't like other people. Tomorrow you may meet some."

Traditionally subsistence hunter-gatherers, the Lepcha lived scattered throughout these foothills and in neighboring Sikkim. After a series of invasions from Tibet and Nepal, the Lepchas' numbers had dwindled to almost nil. I wondered if their shyness was actually due to being nearly wiped out. I'd stay away from people too if they had taken my land and changed my culture.

The afternoon sun was hot. A breeze drifted down the mountain. Along the south-facing slopes, terraces of tea and cardamom had been carved out of the jungle in large green swaths.

Shanti plucked a ripe cardamom from a low bush. "Try one."

I took it, hesitating. It resembled a fig. I chewed slowly. The flavor exploded on my tongue, spicy and sharp, almost like toothpaste.

Shanti huffed and puffed as her flip-flops smacked against her feet. She kept stopping every few minutes for a sip of water. I wanted to rip my arm away and run up the trail, but she kept her grip firm. Her hand felt hot against my skin.

"I think you are very fit, for being American," Shanti said.

"I hike a lot," I said, feeling the urge to apologize. Was she hoping that I would struggle to get up the hill?

At last, we came to a tiny house surrounded by rice paddies.

"Ninda," Shanti said, "we sleep here tonight."

I was still unclear as to what we were doing. Glancing back, I saw that everyone from the bus was lugging suitcases and satchels as they walked. They must be going to the same meeting as us. *A revival meeting in the middle of Lepcha-land? And I'm supposed to be an anthropologist?* Suddenly, I felt weak with despair. I was hot, tired, and sick. And once again, I was a fraud to the people around me.

We put our things in the upstairs loft and came down for lunch. A toothless woman in a red sari ladled out yellow rice and dal spiced with cardamoms. Shanti ate her plate of food and obligingly finished mine.

"You don't each much," she said curiously, studying me over the top of her tin cup.

"I'm not hungry," I said, which was true. I was sick of dal bhat. Nepalis ate dal bhat three times a day, every day without variation. Anything that didn't include rice or lentils wasn't considered food.

Ninda was more of a settlement than a village. Tiny homesteads lay scattered across the hills. Although this was Lepcha-land, the Lepchas lived a day's walk over the mountain ridge in India. Sikkim. Without a special permit, I couldn't cross the border. Luckily for me, many Lepcha were coming for this religious gathering. The Lepcha called themselves Mutanchi Rong, which means "the ravine folk" or "the people who wait for Tashe Ting— the supreme God." I liked both translations. Maybe the meaning had changed along with them switching to Christianity. Today, they were farmers, growing maize, millet, tea, and cardamom. I gazed at the steep green hills. What would it have been like before the terraces and farming? The jungle looked thick and dark from here. It would have been beautiful.

"There's a Lepcha." Shanti pointed.

I almost laughed. Were we Lepcha hunting? It felt ridiculous. To me, everyone looked the same. How could Shanti tell that he was a Lepcha? The man wore simple handspun clothes and a little hat. He looked like all the other traditional people I'd seen over the last few months. I was beginning to understand that although everyone looked the same to me, the differences to those who lived here were enormous. People were not only born into different castes but religions as well. These mountains were home to Tibetan Buddhists, Hindu Nepalis, and recently-turned-Christian Lepchas.

"It's a big problem," Shanti said.

"What is?" I asked. We were walking uphill toward a large tent in a field above the village. A breeze swept along the trail and birds shrieked. The setting sun bathed the hills in golden rays.

"Christian Lepcha cannot marry non-Christian Lepcha. They must marry outside their people." She flicked a fly from her head.

"Doesn't that mean their numbers are dying out even more?"

"I suppose so. You should ask my father about it. He will be happy to meet you."

At the top of the hill, women in bright saris served steaming portions of dal bhat on thick, broad leaves. People stood around, chatting and eating with their fingers, casually letting their leaf plates fall to the ground when they were finished. Shanti and I found a seat near the back of the tent, on the women's side. Like all services in Nepal, women and men sat separately; women on the left and men on the right.

The service began with singing in Nepali. I clapped with the music and closed my eyes when they prayed. Shanti's father stood near the front and spoke loudly so everyone could hear. Since it was all in Nepali, I paid no attention to his words. I took notes in my journal and drew pictures of mountains. I studied the faces around me and smiled at the babies peering over their mother's shoulders.

I had almost dozed off when suddenly I heard Shanti's father say in English, "I am thinking there is someone here who does not understand me."

Everyone turned and stared at me. "This is our little American sister from the United States. She is an anthropologist."

I glanced around sheepishly. My cheeks burned.

"An anthropologist does not just look," he said. "They observe people. They see beyond the surface." Shanti's father went on, mixing English with Nepali so I could understand. For the rest of the sermon, people kept glancing back at me suspiciously, as though I could read their minds. I tried to look attentive and wise.

It was late when Shanti and I got back to the tiny loft. A dozen or so women had already spread out their blankets on the floor. As they combed their long dark hair by candlelight, they laughed and talked like old friends. *Do they know each other? Where are they from?* They looked young. Even the older women had lithe muscles and slim waists.

I lay quietly, listening to their voices rise and fall. Some spoke in low tones. Others seemed to be telling funny stories, their stifled laughter erupting into the night. A baby cried, and a woman put the child to her breast. Someone hushed a toddler. A wind blew through the open window, rattling the dry cornstalks that were piled in the corner.

Pressed together in the tiny hot attic, I felt claustrophobic. Would they ever stop talking? They seemed giddy with the opportunity to be together. It was probably a rare event to be away from their husbands and daily chores, even if it was just for the weekend. I watched them stroke each other's hair and casually hug. Then they curled up on the floor close to each other. It was so different from my background. In the West, touch happened only intentionally and occasionally. I thought about my Swedish relatives. Their love consisted of coffee and pastries and awkward hugs at weddings and funerals. I missed them just the same. No matter how hard I tried, I would never fit completely into this culture.

I spent the following day conducting ethnographic interviews with a curious crowd of onlookers. Anxious to see the anthropologist at work, they swarmed around me. As Lepchas answered my questions, several Nepalis translated for me. The only problem was that they all talked at the same time. The Nepali translators seemed disappointed at my questions regarding childrearing, religion, cultural change, and traditional customs. After a while, my questions sounded silly, even to me. The translators interjected their own ideas and opinions about the Lepcha, which I dutifully wrote down in my notebook.

"No, no," one Nepali man said. "The Lepcha have two or three wives, not one."

"We have one wife now." The Lepcha man shook his head.

"That is not so," the Nepali man insisted. "Two wives." He held up two fingers.

I figured the poor man was talking about their culture today, after Christianity. I felt sorry for the Lepchas, who had come here under such scrutiny. They had round brown faces with felted woolen hats and homespun mountain clothes. They answered slowly and with great consideration, as though they were taking a test. These Lepcha were Christians; most were first generation converts.

"Why did you convert?" I asked.

"Buddhist rituals very hard." The Lepcha man sighed. "Expensive. We must pay lama to make offering. Christianity is simpler."

The translator explained that the rituals in Tibetan Buddhism require specialized lamas and monks. He added that the lamas viewed the Lepcha as inferior because they couldn't read the sacred texts. Christianity offered a simpler religion where they could perform their own rituals and prayers. They could even form their own churches, led by a pastor from their tribe.

"It was difficult at first," the Lepcha man said.

"What was difficult?" I asked.

"Difficult to convert because . . ." He scratched his head. "People were angry."

"People were angry at you for converting?"

"Yes, people made much fun of us. They said we are taking American religion."

I knew that Tibetan Buddhism was also relatively new to the Lepcha. It had been introduced by monks in the 1700s. Prior to this, the Lepcha were animists who believed in nature spirits. The spirits were good or bad, taking care of their livestock or spoiling the crops.

"We used to pray to the evil spirits, not the good ones, because we feared them," a Lepcha man explained. "But now we are not afraid like the old days. With Christianity, we know that those were just superstitions."

Superstitions. The word stuck in my head. I was certainly familiar with superstitions. Charismatic Christians believe in angels, demons, and the Holy Spirit. Catholics pray to dozens of saints. *What is wrong with believing in a waterfall goddess or a mountain god? Isn't it all the same thing?*

That night, we ate dinner again under a tent above the village and listened to long sermons and hours of singing. I picked at my rice and fed it to the dogs when no one could see. Night came, and the first stars appeared. Someone lit a campfire. During a break in the service, we all stood around the fire and warmed ourselves.

"You are Julie?" a young man asked.

He wore a white, long-sleeved shirt tucked into his dress pants. His English sounded beautiful. He introduced himself as Ishor, from Manipur in India, where he attended seminary school. He was with a group of other young men—all missionaries from Manipur. He was funny and smart. I wished I'd met all of them earlier. He talked passionately about social justice, empowerment for marginalized castes like the Lepcha, and the evils of domestic violence.

"Some women are too afraid to come forward," Ishor said. "They have no one in their village who will say that beating is wrong."

"So, what happens to them?" I asked.

"Sometimes they try to escape, go back to their families, but if they have children . . ." He shook his head.

"So, that's why they are the first to convert?"

"Yes, they love Christianity because it teaches that beating is abuse, especially for women and children. We teach love and discipline, but no beating."

"That's good," I said.

Another young man from Ishor's group spoke up. "We also teach that girls should go to school, which is a very radical concept to traditional families."

"Yes." Ishor nodded. "In the Christian households, girls are valued as much as boys."

I remembered that Shanti was the only girl with a job in her village, probably the only one who received a formal education. How lucky she must feel to have a progressive Christian father who valued her as much as his sons.

Suddenly, I felt sad and incredibly lonely. I was an outsider on many levels. Not only was I an American, but Christianity would never be for me what it was for these people. For them it was a way forward, a way to move into the twenty-first century with the positive values and ideologies of Western culture: equality, education, and democracy. For me, Christianity had been something different. It had been rules and patriarchy. *Don't be yourself. Do this, but not that. Think this way, not that way.*

Firelight danced on Ishor's face as he spoke. Stars hung overhead, huge and bright. They looked close enough to touch. Weren't we all made from stardust? Wasn't everything made from the same elements, the ones I struggled to memorize from the periodic table? If we were all the same, why was it so hard to feel a part of things? I didn't fit into my parents' Christianity, and I didn't fit into the Christianity here. I did not fit in anywhere.

I spent the next few days in Lepcha-land with the missionaries. I talked to the boys from Manipur, and they helped to translate my interviews. I learned about the traditional sororate and levirate marriage rules. If a man's wife died, her family was obligated to give him a sister or another woman from within her family. If the husband died, his family was obliged to supply another husband. The systems ensured that there were no single parents. I learned that the Lepcha do not view romantic love the way we do here in America. They view food as the key to someone's heart. When a wife cooks for her husband or when the husband brings home food, their mutual obligations foster feelings of attachment and security, not romantic love. The Lepcha view all relationships as a series of mutual obligations. If you fulfill your role in that relationship, love will eventually grow.

I thought about their system as I packed my bag and prepared to leave. Compared to the peaceful Lepcha, Western notions of romantic love seemed frivolous. Maybe they had a better system. Put two people in a relationship with agreed upon expectations, and long, steadfast attachment would follow. Someday, I hoped to find this kind of love, but I also wanted the romantic kind. Would I ever feel that way about someone?

Waving goodbye to Shanti, I set off down the mountain. Shanti would leave later that day with her father. Everyone packed up and left. Even the Lepcha, with their little satchels and flip-flops, had set off over the mountains and back to their homes.

The morning sun shone bright and hot in a deep-blue sky. I caught the bus down by the river. We lurched away in a cloud of black smoke, the gears grinding as the bus made its way down the winding mountain road. Relieved to be traveling alone after Shanti's nonstop chatter, I stared out the window, relishing the quiet. It was nice not to have to smile or nod or strain to understand what she was saying.

After several hours of winding mountain roads, we arrived in Kakarbhitta, a border town and one of the major trading centers between Nepal and India. Hot, flat, and dusty, it felt like I was on another planet, so different from the green jungles of Lepcha-land. Arab traders with camels roamed the streets. Merchants with turbans, speaking a dozen languages, sold coconuts, pineapples, stereos, CDs, bolts of cloth, and Mickey Mouse stuffed animals.

I was supposed to change buses here. As I staggered into the milieu of donkeys and rumbling diesel engines, I realized I had no idea where to catch the next bus. The town did not seem like the kind of place I wanted to get lost in. For once, I was glad for my dirty-blond hair and sunburned skin. A crowd of eager street boys surrounded me.

"Dharan," I said.

"Ah, Dharan, Dharan. Yes!" They led me through the maze of buses and rickshaws to the opposite end of the station, where a large blue bus sat idling near the gate.

The driver, a thin man with a cigarette and enormous sunglasses, waved me on. I paid my fare and climbed up the ladder to sit in the back. He motioned for me to come up front. I was pleased. Usually this spot was reserved for men who gave the driver beer and cigarettes.

From here, I had a clean, undisturbed view of the road. As we swung away from the station with a lurch, the driver glanced at me from the sides of his reflective glasses. *Is he trying to impress me?* He sat hunched forward, gripping the large steering wheel, jerking the bus around carts, donkeys, and cattle. Every time we overtook another bus, he honked madly, swerving into the opposite lane to pass. We careened around potholes, rickshaws, and bicycles. We were going fast. Too fast. I clutched my backpack and held on to my seat to avoid hitting my head on the ceiling. The driver grinned madly. He pressed down on the accelerator. Now, I knew he was trying to scare me. He was doing a good job.

Halfway to Dharan, we stopped at a check post where the driver disappeared into a nondescript government building. We waited for ages. *What is he doing?* I looked around. All the passengers were asleep or brushing away flies. They appeared unconcerned.

When the man returned, he'd forgotten his sunglasses. His eyes were wide and glassy. His shirt was unbuttoned. His face twitched. Was he angry or high? Twice he killed the engine as we maneuvered back onto the road. By now, two more men had joined me in the front of the cab. They exchanged glances, smiling as though it were a great joke. Weaving over the road, the driver cursed. Sweat dripped from his temples. Trees, cows, children, and women flashed by as we came up behind another bus. The driver jerked the wheel and hit the accelerator. He waved angrily as the other driver gestured for us to slow down. We pulled into the opposite lane to pass. Suddenly, we were neck and neck with the other bus, flying around a blind corner. Ahead, I saw an oncoming military truck, a cow, and three rickshaws. I squeezed my eyes shut, waiting for the impact.

The impact hit, shoving me into the side window. I looked up. We had only grazed the other bus. The other driver hit the gas, pulling ahead. Our driver hit his head against the windshield. He was angry. Blood dripped from his forehead.

I froze, hardly daring to breathe, wondering what to do. He muttered to himself and wiped his brow. I could smell sweat and alcohol from across the aisle. I sank into my seat, praying he wouldn't look at me.

By the time we reached Dharan, I was shaking so hard I didn't notice the man who had seated himself next to me. Everyone was getting off the bus, but the man blocked my way.

"Excuse me." I tried to stand up.

"Wait, sister." Beads of sweat stood out on his upper lip. His large frame filled the tiny seat. "Tell me, where are you from?"

"America," I said. "I need to go."

"Where are you going?"

"Kathmandu. Excuse me." Again, I attempted to get around him.

"But there are no buses tonight . . . you must come with me."

"I know where I'm staying tonight. I'll leave in the morning. Please, I need to go." I tried to shove past him, but he pushed me down.

"I own this bus. Sit." He spoke slowly, his face dark and unkind. "Where do you stay tonight?"

"With friends."

"Maybe I know them?"

"I don't think so."

"Do you have a ticket?"

"Yes," I lied, shaking.

"Show me."

"It's not with me."

"Ah, you need a new ticket. Come with me."

As if on cue, the bus driver gunned the engine. We swerved down a side street. Panicking, I glanced around. I was the only passenger on the bus. The driver smirked from behind his dark sunglasses.

"Here is *my* house." The man rose, gripping my arm.

We were stopped in front of a gated white house. The man twisted my arm and pulled me off the bus.

"My friends are waiting for me!" I shouted, glancing around the empty street. I had no idea where I was. Ignoring me, the man pushed through a large metal gate and into the lower level of the house. Inside, the room was surprisingly spacious and cool. Ornate rugs covered the floor before a large, official-looking desk. The man went to the desk and picked up the telephone. He spoke rapidly in Nepali. At last, he turned to me, smiling.

"You must be here at nine o' clock to pick up your ticket."

"Why can't I have it now?" I asked.

"It must be delivered tomorrow morning. You come back then."

"No." I turned to leave.

The man insisted. "You must buy. Otherwise, no ticket—no bus."

"Okay, fine." I frowned.

"You pay now."

Furious, I fumbled in my purse for two hundred rupees.

"Now, we will have tea." The man rang a little bell.

Tea? *Is he crazy?* I didn't want tea. It was almost dark outside. I needed to get to the missionary base. "No, thank you," I said.

An older woman in a blue sari appeared with a tray of tea. She set it down with a thump on his desk.

"This is my first wife," the man said, smiling. "I want you to meet her. Maybe I call your father and ask for you."

Ask for me? Ask what? I tried to smile.

"Would you like to be my wife?" The man lit a cigarette and inhaled.

"No." I shook my head firmly. "I am a student. In America, we go to school."

"Yes, yes." The man glanced at the older woman, who looked at me with pity.

"But you could be my wife. Tell me, what is your telephone number at home?"

I almost laughed, but the situation wasn't funny. It felt unreal. I made up a number and wrote it down. The man nodded thoughtfully and tapped the paper. *Is he trying to kidnap me?* I finished my tea and tried to keep my legs from shaking.

He turned to his wife. She shook her head as she glanced at me. "Just wait here." The man stood and walked into the next room.

Without thinking, I sprang to my feet and bolted for the front door. I ran through the gate and out into the street. "Julie!" I heard the man call from behind, but I kept going. When I got to the corner, I glanced back. He was nowhere to be seen. I forced myself to walk. My legs were trembling. I kept expecting him to appear any minute and drag me back to his house.

It was dark. Up ahead I could see car lights and trucks going by, but my sense of direction failed me. I walked quickly toward the lights, jumping at the sound of dogs snarling behind gates and men coughing in the shadows. Just as I reached the main road, I heard someone calling my name.

"Julie! Julie!" It was Obed.

I cried with relief.

"Where have you been, Julie?" Obed hurried up to me, looking concerned and exasperated.

"I don't know." I tried to explain about the bus driver and the man who made me go to his house to buy the ticket, but it came out jumbled and bizarre. Obed shook his head.

"I know of that man." He took my backpack and maneuvered us along the narrow sidewalk. "He's no good. I will go with you in the morning to get your bus ticket." He muttered something under his breath, which I couldn't quite hear. I trotted along beside him in the dark, happy to be found.

CHAPTER EIGHTEEN

◁❑◘❑◉❑◉❑◉❑◉❑◘◘❑▷

AS IT TURNED OUT, I did not leave the next day. Not surprisingly, there was something amiss with the bus ticket I purchased. Obed went alone to the man's house and came back fuming. I had to wait another two days before returning to Kathmandu. I was pleased. I spent my time at the base reading about the Lepcha, taking notes, and hanging out with the girl students. They took me shopping and played pop songs on their tiny tape recorder.

Obed quizzed me on what I had found. He knew quite a bit about the indigenous groups of Sikkim and Nagaland, but he seemed hesitant to say what he thought.

"How does missionary work affect these people?" I asked.

"It's complicated," he said slowly. "During the time of colonialism, they were made to feel backwards, uneducated."

"You mean marginalized?"

"Yes, marginalized. And there was a lot of racial superiority and abuse. But in the Lepcha case, it wasn't just from the British missionaries, it was also from Tibetan immigrants and Nepalis moving into Sikkim. Because they are, how do you say?"

"Indigenous?"

"Yes, the first people, they were always at the bottom."

I told him about the Lepcha man and his comment that people made fun of him when he converted to Christianity and that he was taking up an American religion.

Obed nodded. "I know this is a big problem for converts. But you know, Christianity should not come to people as an American or English religion. It should come from within the culture."

"But do you think it's even good to change the culture?" I asked, hardly daring to voice my own inner conflict.

Obed was thoughtful. He gazed across the field behind our compound before answering. "I think," he said, "that people will always want to better their lives. You cannot tell people that it's good to change or good to stay the same. People want to be like successful people. A better life for their children. To have electricity and television. They want a Western education. Who are we to tell them they should remain barefoot, hungry, or worshiping their traditional gods?"

"I think it's sad that the whole world is changing and these cultures are dying out." I fingered the hem of my dress. The late afternoon sun beat down, hot and bright. From the neighbor's backyard, I could hear children playing and goats bleating in the distance.

"I agree," Obed said. Leaning back against the wall, he pushed his glasses up on his nose and told me about his childhood. He was the son of a government minister who taught agricultural training in remote villages. As his father was gone most of the time, Obed and his brothers grew up in boarding schools. He went to college in Nagaland and then volunteered with a mission's organization in India for two years before being called to Nepal.

"How did you know you were *called*?" I told him about the missionary kids from Colorado and how each of them seemed to have daily conversations with a god who told them who to marry, where to go, and what to do.

Obed nodded. "I think many times people want so much to hear God or have a religious experience that they read divine will into their own ideas or thoughts. I do this sometimes because maybe I want a certain person to be God's will, but it doesn't always work."

"So, how does God speak to you? Did he tell you to come to Nepal from Nagaland?"

Obed laughed. "No, God doesn't hold great conversations with me. My grandparents are from Nepal, and I wanted to research my family roots and see where I was from. It was pretty simple. But I think God puts those desires in your heart if they are of Him."

We both fell silent. A fly landed on my leg. I shook it off. I thought about God's calling or divine will. A lump formed in my throat. Since India, I had wanted so much to feel one way or the other, either to be a Christian or to be something else. But I was torn. I wanted to feel a greater purpose to my life, but what? And from whom? I had trouble believing in the existence of God, much less having daily revelations . . . and yet.

Why did Obed find me in the street running from that crazy old man? Why did Chris appear in Solu Khumbu when I was sick? How did I come across the French group the afternoon I got lost in the mountains? Was all of that just chance? Did it even matter? Maybe not.

In the evening, I sat next to Obed on the patio with our plates of dal bhat.

"Julie," Obed said, looking at me.

"Yes?"

"You need to eat. It is," he said, then paused to search for the right words, "rude to waste food when there are so many who need it."

My face flamed. He was right. How rude I had been. Maybe someday I could give up my quest for thinness. Who would I be without worrying about my weight? I didn't even know. Would anyone like me? Where would I fall on the scale of beauty? What was beauty anyway? Did it lie inside me, and if so, could I find it? Could I make friends with it? Could I be okay with myself?

"I'm sorry." I looked down at my plate. Obed said nothing but lightly touched my hand. It felt like forgiveness. I took a bite of the rice.

That night, I lay looking at the stars from the window and listening to dogs bark in the distance. The air was fragrant with the scent of jasmine and cooking fires. It was colder now, the end of November. Tomorrow, I would go back to Kathmandu. In another week, I would return home to snow and Christmas and family. I felt full for the first time in weeks, maybe ever.

In the morning, I couldn't find Obed. I was miserable at the thought that I might leave without seeing him. The girls from the base all gathered around me, holding my hands and braiding my hair. They whispered together about my bare legs and dirty-blond hair. I liked them. *I could do this*, I thought suddenly. *I could come back and live here and be a missionary, of sorts.* Could I really? I didn't know. It was almost time to go.

Just as I was gathering my pack, Obed appeared. He looked disheveled and nervous. Awkwardly, he took my hand and shook it, murmuring something about being glad to have met me. Then he slipped an envelope and a small brown package into my hands and disappeared.

I glanced down at the package. The paper was thin, like newsprint. Nestled amongst the folds lay a string of sky-blue beads, the kind women wore once they married. They were the color of the blue forget-me-nots in my mother's flower beds. They reminded me of the sky in Solu Khumbu. Under the beads lay a postcard with a picture of Mount Everest, snowy and dark. On the back he had written:

Thank you, Julie, for the talks we have had.
May you be safe in your travels,
and may the Lord's guidance
be the source of your strength
in your dreams and journeys.
Love, Obed.

I stood in the hot sun, looking down at the card. Tears pricked my eyelids. The sun shone. Trucks roared. Children cried.

B. B. Rai arrived to see me off. He tied my pack on the back of his motorcycle. I waved goodbye to the young girls and the shy Korean guy. I looked back one last time at the small blue house where somewhere in the kitchen rice was cooking and prayers were being whispered in a dozen languages. Then we rumbled out in a cloud of fumes and dust.

At the station, B.B. Rai helped me locate my bus. I put my backpack on my seat before saying goodbye.

"All set?" B.B. Rai smiled down at me. The sun reflected off his glasses.

I stood, looking up at him. Bus engines shook the ground. In the distance, I could see India, golden and flat, stretching out beyond the city.

"I think it will be alright for you now," he said gravely, but his eyes smiled.

"Thank you," I said. Part of me wondered if I would ever come back. Maybe I would enroll in language classes in Kathmandu or live in a village and work in an orphanage. Maybe I would come back. Maybe Obed would ask me to marry him. For a moment, I imagined myself walking through the gate of the little house as a wife—a missionary's wife.

Then the image passed.

I would never come back, just as I would never be a Buddhist nun in Junbesi or a Christian the way my parents wanted me to be. My path lay elsewhere. The good way, I thought. I would find the good way for me. Not for anyone else. It would be my way, my ancient path. Swallowing back the lump in my throat, I shook B.B. Rai's hand. "I think it will be too."

Later, flying out of Kathmandu on a morning in early December, I remembered his words: "I think it will be alright for you now."

I leaned my head against the seat, exhausted. *Will it be alright? Will I be alright? Will I be able to navigate the changes of my life? Growing up, falling in love, children, a career, and what about old age? What will hold me together when everything else falls apart?*

At the moment, I didn't know, but looking out the window of that plane as the mountains sank away beneath me, I felt a sense of peace. Something in me was finally growing up.

Yes, I thought. I would be okay. Perhaps the missionaries in Dharan knew more about me than I did about myself. Perhaps they could see a young girl moving from one cosmology, one way of looking at the world, to another. I thought I was looking for the Jirels and the Lepchas, but I was really looking for myself. They knew I would never return to be a missionary. It didn't matter. They had given me the gift of faith. Not faith in religion, but faith in the future. Faith in the unseen. Faith in the ability to weather my life.

EPILOGUE

◁❙▢◉❙▢❙◉❙◉❙◉❙▢❙◉▢❙▷

BUTTER LAMPS BURN ON the altar before me. A giant Buddha statue smiles down as I kneel on the floor, head bowed. Tears run down my cheeks. I wipe them away, aware that some Sikh men are looking at me. I'm at a temple in Ladakh, India, with a group of students studying Himalayan culture and ecology. I'm almost forty years old.

In three weeks, I will return home to my daughters and fiancé. Our wedding is the Saturday after I return. There is no word for divorce in Ladakhi. They don't understand the concept here. Palden, the village chief, tells everyone that I'm the anthropologist with two husbands. They understand that, as most families practice polyandry, a form of marriage where two brothers marry one woman.

I remember my first trip to the Himalayas so very long ago. I didn't know then that things would fall apart. There would be cancer and fires, divorce and children, a husband, and love lost and then found again. It would take years to fully leave the Christian church, and even more years to find my people outside of religion. At nineteen, I didn't want to leave my parents behind. It turned out that I didn't have to. We found common ground in being a family.

Over time, I had children of my own. There were birthday parties and Christmases and family dinners. My sister and I would work out a relationship based on books and our mutual love for our daughters. For a time, we would live next door to each other. Like the Lepcha, I would have a home within the mutual bonds of obligation and family. Then, that too, would change. I would remarry and make different friends. Jobs would change. Businesses would fail.

Incense rises into the air. I breathe deeply, savoring the aroma of sandalwood and juniper. The fortune teller was right. I had a good life. It was full of surprises. I had two more great loves. And, two beautiful daughters. I whisper a prayer for them. I'm probably praying what every mother prays: that my daughters will have long lives. That I will live to see them grow. That someday I can let them go and live their own lives. Maybe even let go of mine.

Rain, silence, mountains. Snow, trails, heat. This is all there is. Is it enough? The words of Jeremiah come back to me: *Ask for the ancient paths. Ask where the good way is and walk in it, and you will find rest for your soul.* I have asked for the ancient paths. I have found the good way. Suddenly, I find myself smiling. Wonder. Joy. Peace. Hindus call it *ananda*—the joy that holds the universe together. When things fall apart, this is what remains. This love. This beautiful planet. The faith of the mountains, which remind me of where I came from and where one day, I will return.

ACKNOWLEDGEMENTS

Many thanks to everyone who made this book possible. To Lee Montgomery who helped me realize which story I was trying tell, and to Lynn Moon who worked tirelessly with me week after week. Thank you, Lynn for pushing me to tell the story better. To John, at Koehler Books, who believed in me, even when I did not, and to my dear friend, James Donaldson who helped me find my voice years ago. Thank you to all the people who hosted me so graciously twenty years ago in Nepal, particularly the missionaries in Dharan. I have never met more generous people. Finally, my gratitude and thanks go to my husband, Todd, who told me to get on with this book once and for all because life was too short. I love you.

CPSIA information can be obtained
at www.ICGtesting.com
Printed in the USA
LVHW111258050320
649092LV00006B/42